MW00711961

TERROR
unprecedented

Where: United States of America

When: Soon, Very Soon

How: Nuclear Bomb

Why: Find Out in This Book

By

Olusegun Masha
(An Ex-Muslim)

TERROR unprecedented

COPYRIGHT © 2007, 2008 BY SEGUN MASHA
ALL RIGHTS RESERVED.

No portion of this book may be reproduced, stored in a retrieval system, or transmitted in any form or by any means- electronic, mechanical, photocopy, recording, or any other, without the prior written permission from Olusegun Masha.

Unless otherwise indicated, Scripture quotations are taken from The Holy Bible King James Version and Revised Standard Version on the E-Sword Bible software, copyright 2001 Rick Meyers.

All references to Greek or Hebrew word definitions are from Strong Bible Dictionary contained in the E-Sword Bible software, copyright 2001 Rick Meyers.

We publicly acknowledge many facts and figures reproduced in this book as originally published by their original authors or publishers as stated.

ISBN: 0-9755927-6-9
ISBN 13: 978-0-9755927-6-2
Includes bibliographical references.

Library of Congress Catalogue of Numbers: 2007928209

Published in 2007, 2008 by Church Without Walls Publications, USA.

TABLE OF CONTENT

This book is dedicated to all those who will hear the message and act appropriately to escape the wrath to come.

::CHAPTER ONE

INTRODUCTION:
END OF THE AGE

December 31, 2007, Atlanta Georgia:
As the year came to an end, I visited a Prayer-Garden in Alpharetta Georgia (for its serene atmosphere) to pray and to seek the face of the Lord. I arrived Sunday evening at about 6:45 p.m. and went straight to bed because I was tired. I awoke at about 12:59 a.m., prayed and studied for a while, and then went back to sleep around 4:45 a.m. It was then the Lord showed me this vision:

I was walking on the street on what seemed to be a normal day when suddenly I heard a resounding shout of Hallelujah! Hallelujah! Hallelujah! from heaven. The shout, obviously of angels, probably hundreds of thousands of them, sounded as one; like a song, sweet, yet so powerful and deliberate, as in proclaiming an important event or era. So I looked, and there it was, just as I had seen it before- a vision of devastation; of calamities- people disappearing, building collapsing, earth-shaking, people running, crisis everywhere. My attention was particularly drawn to the specific events and scenes as they played-out, one after the other, in an exact manner and sequence, just as I had seen them play-out before. I knew the end had come; the end of the world. And so I began to explain to the people that the end of the world had come with the promised wrath of God being poured out on the rebellious people left behind. I was saved and safe, but many were not. Confidently I explained what was going on to the people; and I was very calm until I remembered my brother, my own blood brother, who happens to be a

Muslim. I remembered that I had preached the Gospel to him a number of times, and he had flatly refused the gift of Salvation that came through Jesus Christ- the savior of the world. In agony I cried out loud for his soul.

> **I COULD NOT STOMACH THE FACT THAT MY BLOOD BROTHER WOULD END UP IN HELL IF THE EVENT TIMES-OUT ON HIM.**

I could not stomach the fact that my own brother would end up in hell if that event timed-out on him. In desperation, I asked for a cell-phone to call my brother to see if he was still alive, so I can ask him to repent and receive Jesus Christ before it's too late. I became desperately concerned for him and other Muslims who have rejected the grace of God, and have refused to be saved and restored to God through Jesus Christ.

Still in the vision, I ran up and down the street wondering what to do. Then suddenly it came to me, "My Book! My Book!", I exclaimed as I remembered my then unpublished book, Terror Unprecedented. At that, a deep sense of regret came upon me as I realized that I should have made efforts to publish the book for all to read and understand that we are now in the end-times. I realized that my book would have helped the millions, probably billions, of people to better understand the signs of the times, know what was coming, and then make up their *own minds whether to receive Jesus and be saved or reject Him and be damned. A very heavy burden came upon my heart because it was my express failure to push-hard for the release of the book that caused the people to die without the grace of God. Meaning, I will be held responsible for their blood even as they go to hell en mass. At that, I woke up, very frightened.*

So what is it about this book that I am compelled to write that you may read?

The meaning of the vision is very clear: get the book out or be held responsible for the blood of hundreds of thousands and millions of Muslims (and others) who die ignoring the saving grace of our Lord Jesus Christ. I don't consider myself to be a professional writer; I simply write whenever I feel the need to write. I did not receive any formal training in *Writing*, and I do not have any ghost writers. As a young man in High School and University, I often wrote long essays and theses, but nothing out of the ordinary. On my Investment Banking job, I often wrote internal memos, letters, and proposals; nothing extra-ordinary. And as a Minister of the Gospel, writing down important information, dreams, and visions with specific dates and time became absolutely necessary primarily for reference purposes. It never for once crossed my mind that I would, one day, write a book for all to read. But one event led to another, and now here I am, compelled to write to you.

The crash of the *Space Shuttle Columbia* literally forced me to write this book. Although I was very hesitant at the start for I did not know how well I could truthfully write about a sensitive subject such as this one without offending anyone. The thought of answering questions posed by spiritually blind intellectuals, secularized church-folks, and angry Muslims sometimes made my heart-beat to skip. And so with much fear and reluctance, I carefully considered every word and phrase that I would use to communicate a very difficult but important subject of which I have limited knowledge.

As I began to write, my whole destiny began to unfold before me. The Lord began to speak to me through the life of Moses: like Moses, who was raised in the house of Pharaoh, escaped death, and came back to set his people free from Pharaoh's bondage, so was I raised in a Moslem home; then saved by Jesus Christ [escaped death (hell)], and now being sent back by the Lord to release my brothers and sisters from the bondage of Islam.

For the purpose of this book, the Lord made many things about my life (past, present, and future) to become very clear to me. He showed me that my name "Olusegun" or "Oluwasegun" (elongated version) *means the Victory of Jesus Christ*; and through a dear friend fluent in the Hebrew language, the Lord also revealed to me that my last name "Masha", spelt "Moshe" in Hebrews, means *Moses*. But despite these great insights and understanding, I couldn't get past the fear of offending the Muslims and rousing the anger of Islamic radicals. Whenever I remembered the worldwide riots sparked by the *Mohammed Cartoons*, my heart-beat skipped a bit; thus I was not at all motivated to write this book. I begged God to give the assignment to well-known preachers like Benny Hinn and T.D. Jakes, but the Lord insisted I was born for this very purpose. And so I proceeded to write, but my attitude towards the project was wrong. I made quite an effort to make my writing socially acceptable and politically correct. I even thought about omitting my name from the book to make me anonymous in order to protect myself from possible harm.

To make the matter worse, I approached some so-called Christian publishers for help. They flatly rejected my manuscript on the ground that it was too "deep" for a modern society like America. They suggested I delete all the *dreams, visions, and Scriptures*, and fashion the book to appeal to a larger secular America. To them, the more watered-down my message is, the more money I will make. They said if I ever want to be successful as a writer, my book must not address "sin or hell" or anything of that sort until I have become known and respected, like T. D. Jakes and Joyce Meyer are, then I can begin to write some serious stuff. In one "organized" church in Atlanta, two of their so-called prophetesses bounced my manuscript back and forth for about six weeks, and then told me it's not worth pursuing. All hell broke loose on me because of this book. The pressure was on for me to water-down the message. I even came up with a very friendly and less dramatic title, all in a bid to down-tone the message. But this greatly displeased the Lord, to the point where He had to, again, appear to me in order to put the matter to rest:

March 2004:

I had a vivid dream in which I saw the Lord Jesus Christ give me a bowl of chicken and a cup of seasoning, and said to me, "cook; let my people eat." I put the bowl of chicken on the stove, but I diluted the seasoning with water before I used it. When the food was ready, I called out, and the people showed up to eat. But when they saw the food, they rejected it. Although to me, the food was good enough, to the people, it was not. And so with a broken-heart, I went to the Lord and asked why I was rejected. He did not say a word; He simply gave me another bowl of chicken and another cup of seasoning, and said to me, "cook, let my people eat." Again I put the bowl of chicken on the stove, and diluted the seasoning before use. When the food was ready, the people again rejected it. Then a painful sense of rejection and pur-poselessness gripped my heart, and I began cry. I turned to the Lord and asked Him why this was happening to me. He looked at me sternly and said, "If you dilute my Word, I will destroy your ministry and render your life useless..."

At once I realized that the food is the Gospel message, even this book, which I am called to bring to the nations. Diluting the seasoning amounts to watering-down the message to entreat carnality, and avoid persecution and criticisms. If the salt (seasoning) loses its flavor, how shall it be seasoned? It is then good for nothing but to be thrown out and trampled underfoot (Matthew 5:13).

I repented and asked the Lord to change my heart and make me bold to do His will.
Unfortunately, many ministers of the Gospel have diluted the integrity of God's Word for this very reason. Many others have diluted God's message for the sake of money, fame, and worldly gains, thus rendering the message ineffectual, lacking conviction, devoid of persuasion, and no revelation knowledge. So in order to protect the integrity of God's word and message in this book, I decided to self-edit and self-publish it; trusting God to bless it for your sake, and protect me from harm. Scripture clearly shows that our battle is not against flesh and blood (human beings), but against Satan and unseen forces of darkness that rule in the hearts of men, blinding their understanding to the truth:

> **2 Corinthians 4:3-5:** *But if our gospel be hid, it is hid to them that are lost: In whom the god of this world hath blinded the minds of them which believe not, lest the light of the glorious gospel of Christ, who is the image of God, should shine unto them. For we preach not ourselves, but Christ Jesus the Lord; and ourselves your servants for Jesus' sake.*

The mandate of God upon my life is thus:

> **Acts 26:17-19:** *I will deliver you from the Jewish people, as well as from the Gentiles, to whom I now] send you, to open their eyes, in order to turn them from darkness to light, and from the power of Satan to God, that they may receive forgiveness of sins and an inheritance among those who are sanctified by faith in Me.*

My destiny, therefore, as a man set free from the bondage of Islam, is to bring freedom to my Muslim brothers and sisters who are bound just like I was once bound. I am called to speak the truth in the love of God, but to boldly confront religious lies and deceptions. The Bible says, you shall know the truth and the truth shall make you free (John 8:32). I know that many nominal Christians will probably curse me out and accuse me of creating hatred between Muslims and Christians, but I will continue to speak the truth boldly and lovingly because I desire to see millions of Muslims delivered from darkness and set free by the Power of Christ. For their sake, I made a decision to write boldly and lovingly with the hope that God will use this message to save and deliver millions households from the coming wrath. *Terror unprecedented*, therefore, is a book for which only God takes credit. It is purposed to draw your attention to what God has drawn my attention. So please understand that I have not brought you this message by my own power, wisdom, or holiness; but by the grace of the Almighty God.

::CHAPTER TWO

COMPELLED TO
SPEAK OUT

12:45 p.m., February 2, 2003:

The week, up to that Friday, had been a relatively busy one for me. So I decided to put in a couple of hours that Saturday to clear out my desk. However, on my way to the office on *Lawrenceville Highway 29*, my thought was rudely interrupted by the news that the Space Shuttle *Columbia* had met with an accident, and had disintegrated, killing the seven astronauts on board. The news so grieved my heart that I pulled the car over to a *Kroger* gas station for a while to regain my comportment.

Indeed a loss that tragic could bring much grief to the heart, but my anguish of that moment came out of a much deeper concern for the entire American people. Why? Because on March 8, 2002 @ 4:30 a.m., I saw a prophetic vision in which *the Space Shuttle Columbia fell from the sky, broke into pieces, and never rose again.*

That the Shuttle Columbia would crash and all the Astronauts on board would die was made known to me by the Lord Jesus Christ almost a year earlier, but I couldn't do a thing to prevent the tragedy from happening. The fate of the Space Shuttle Columbia was sealed. I discussed this peculiar vision with a number of trusted friends here in the United States as well as in England. I also wrote the message down in my journal and prayed over it as I do with other explicit revelations from the Lord. Although there was no doubt in my mind that this vision was a desolation signal, I did not pay much attention to it afterward. However, on that fateful afternoon of February 2, 2003, I came to the chilling conclusion that the vision concerning *the Space Shuttle Columbia* had definitely come to pass.

As I resumed my trip to the office, pondering the whole incident, a number of questions began to run through my mind: Why was the incident revealed to me ahead of time? Was there anything else I could have done, apart from praying? Did I even pray enough? As these questions ran through my mind, a feeling of guilt tried to overwhelm me, but I quickly got hold of myself. I had to encourage myself in the Lord,

I SAW A VISION IN WHICH THE SHUTTLE COLUMBIA FELL FROM THE SKY, ONE YEAR BEFORE IT ACTUALLY HAPPENED.

reminding myself that my primary responsibility was to pray. I understood that I had no control of the outcome of my prayer; for only God determines the outcome of prayers and petitions. I realized that the impending crash of the Shuttle was revealed to me as a prophetic signal, not so that I can change its outcome, but to prepare my heart for a destiny assignment for which I was born.

The Shuttle represents the glory of America. Prophetically, it also represents an era- the American Era; and its subsequent fall signals the coming end of the Era.

My concern soon shifted from the crashed *Shuttle* to *what the future holds* for America. I was now faced with the grim reality that other important *beyond-the-ordinary* visions that I had seen concerning America may soon come to pass. It is now only a matter of time before other possible grievous incidents, even of greater proportion, begin to happen. At that, a feeling of compassion and responsibility began to well up within me for the sake of the American people.

:: A TOUGH REALITY

The crash of *Shuttle Columbia* was a tough reality for me: it re-echoes the authenticity of God's prophetic word to me particularly regarding America's future- *a future now seriously threatened by Nuclear Attack.* And more so because I am now compelled to proclaim the reality of this prophetic message before the American people and the whole world.

In this book, you will read about a *Coalition* masterminded by a core of three key *individuals.* As revealed to me by the Spirit of God, the leader of the *Trio* is one whose depiction is consistent with that of a ruling *President* of a powerful country- *one with nuclear arsenal.* I find it particularly interesting that this mystery *President*, obviously the leader of the three, has a military posture even though he appears to the world as a civilian President. I believe that this President has a deep-rooted anti-God philosophy or belief, and his bitterness towards America has fueled his resolve to assist the other two (who appeared more like civilians) with nuclear weapons to further their Jihad crusade against America and Israel. For in the vision, I saw the mystery *President* sign a pact with these two men to provide them with a nuclear bomb. I assure you that their evil plan is about to hatch.

:: INTENSE VISIONS OF WAR

Up until the end of 1999, most of the prophetic visions and dreams I had seen and actively shared with

AMERICA'S FUTURE IS NOW SERIOUSLY THREATENED BY NUCLEAR ATTACK

people amounted to important messages that guided and edified individuals, friends, families, churches and corporate entities mostly in their pursuit of purpose and destiny. However, as we crossed the threshold from the 20th Century into the 21st, I began to experience an upward shift in the dimensions, intensity, and rapidity of these prophetic messages. As the intensity of the visions increased, so were the raw images of war, violence, hunger, famine, bloodshed, and all manner of disasters even as they now appear daily on our TV screens.

I assure you that *the wars and rumors of wars, terrors and rumors of terrors, nation rising against nation, great earth-*

quakes and tsunamis in diverse places; famines and pesti-lences; floods and Global Warming signs from the atmo-sphere are, in themselves, not the end. Rather, they are signals of the coming desolations- *the birth-pains of an imminent end* (Luke 21). These I have carefully described in this book with the hope that you will carefully read, and be wise in your judgment and decision.

:: MESSAGE TO THE WHITE HOUSE

As time went by, the Lord compelled me to relate some of these prophetic messages to the White House. And so on April 4, 2003, at about 3:00 a.m., I sent an e-mail to President George W. Bush to thank him for his efforts in combating terrorism, and also to warn him about the impending nuclear attack on America. In the message, I

THE WARS AND RUMORS OF WARS, TERRORS, EARTH-QUAKES AND TSUNAMIS ARE BIRTH-PAINS OF AN IMMINENT END

shared several applicable portions of my *prophecy jour-nal,* and suggested a few counter-terrorism measures to help the nation prepare for the inevitable. I also suggest-ed a number of response strategies to help safeguard our welfare in the face a nuclear holocaust. In writing to the President, I basically called on the President to:

- Special-guard such important but obvious terror targets such as nuclear power plants, water reservoirs, oil reservoirs, refineries, government/military sites, and airports so that they will not constitute sitting ducks for terrorists.
- Partner with allies and other oil producing nations including Nigeria, to guarantee supply in the US in times of serious emergency.
- Begin preliminary work on processing US crude oil reserve and to pursue alternative energy prospects.
- Partner with the Church and work out modalities by which the surpluses of the United States Dept. of Agriculture may be channeled to churches to meet community needs. These churches will serve as Cities of Refuge in time of serious emergency.
- Position fighter jets to guard civilian jetliners during their national and international flights; and to fully secure all airports.

It is now over four years since I sent the e-mail to the White House. For the record, several developments, worthy of enumeration, have taken place since I sent the message to the White House:

- Armed plain-clothed *U.S. Marshals* now accompany local and international flights;
- U.S. Lawmakers approved legislations to allow some level of domestic oil drilling/processing in Alaska, United States;

- President Bush visited Nigeria July 11, 2003. President Bush's visit to Nigeria had *Oil* written all over it as he was accompanied by the then National Security Advisor, Condoleezza Rice- a former board member of Chevron. Flanked by a large entourage of oil executives, the President also met with the executives of Exxon-Mobil, Shell Petroleum, Chevron, Texaco, and others in Nigeria.

Although, on August 8, 2006, a Nigerian Newspaper, *Daily Sun Newspaper,* confirmed that U.S. officials are looking towards Nigeria's oil to avert a potential fuel/energy crisis, I cannot say for sure that my message to the White House has prompted any specific legislations or security measures. Still, it was quite a relief for me to share the information with the White House, for it can be very comforting when you sense that a disaster is about to happen and you are able to warn people ahead of time, so they can take necessary precautions to avert the disaster or reduce its impact.

This book, therefore, is written with you in mind: to share with you what I have been privileged to see and hear in the spirit, and to empower you to walk in the true Victory and Protection that only God Almighty provides. It is also my hope and prayer that the information in this book will impart you with understanding and insight into the mind, motivation, and machination of the terrorists who have sworn to destroy America at all costs. The incidents of 9/11 and *Katrina* are essential reminders of America's vulnerability to disasters orchestrated either from the outside or initiated from within. So I encourage you, once again, to please listen for the perfect will of God for your life even as you read through the pages of this book.

::CHAPTER THREE

RIPPLE EFFECTS
OF 9/11

:: PRE-EMPTIVE STRIKE

Pre-emptive Strike is a policy to attack a perceived enemy in his own land before he attacks you. And you can use nuclear weapons to get the job done if necessary.

The grave incidents *9/11* and *Katrina* remain painful reminders that Americans are vulnerable even in their own land. Not only that, *9/11* indeed caused the nation's policy to rapidly shift from defense to offense. In other words, America's thinking changed from just defending itself against external aggression to *going on the offense against any individual or nation that seem to threaten the national security.* To forestall another *9/11*, the U.S. government will gladly engage in a pre-emptive strike on any nation perceived as an enemy and a threat.

Not only did 9/11 change the mindset of America, it also changed the way the rest of the world's super powers think. *Pre-emptive Strike* is now a widespread policy as many super-power nations (as well as those aspiring to be) gear-up to vigorously protect their interests from external aggressions.

February 2, 2006:
U.S. Intelligence Chief John Negroponte, expressing deep concerns about US security, told the U.S. Senate that relations between Washington and Moscow may become even more difficult in the coming years.

You may not really appreciate what the intelligence Chief was saying here unless you understand that super power nations, especially Russia and China, have rapidly changed their policies and stance to prepare for a major Global Conflict that international diplomacy will never be able to resolve. This Conflict has been clearly prophesied in the Bible some 2500 years ago; the beginning of which we are now experiencing. And so I do not think that it will be unreasonable for me to announce to you that the Third and *Grand Final* World War has already begun. And Yes I do see some key players such as Al-Qaeda and Iran, and a couple of others, all shrouded in the cloak of Islam, ready to drag the whole world into something never before experienced by man— *a terror unprecedented.*

Yet, I see another figure on the horizon: someone much more powerful, influential, and far more strategic in his approach. You can believe what you want to believe, but there is no question in my mind that the people that are set to attack America have already acquired the nuclear bomb. Let me put it this way: if they have not already acquired the bomb, they will surely have the capability to do so. And so, to me, the issue is not if, but when the weapons will be used.

There are speculations that the next time a nuclear bomb goes off, it will be in Israel. But I beg to differ in the matter. For while I recognize the unending battle in the Middle East over who owns Jerusalem, I also recognize the fact that anti-American sentiment has grown quite remarkably in the Middle East and among Muslims in general. The truth is, as much as many Muslims would like to see the Jews wiped out from the face of the earth, they still have America to contend with. And as their contempt for America is a matter of public knowledge, so is their death threat. But for them to really destroy Israel, they have to first find a way to incapacitate America. This is partly the reason why America is now the prime target of the enemy.

:: DEMANDING AMERICA'S DESTRUCTION

December 26, 2002:
The moderator of the radical Islamist Internet Forum *Al-Mojahedoon.Net,* Abu Shihab Al-Qandahari, published an article titled, *The nuclear war is the solution for the destruction of the United States.* To many Americans who read the article, Al-Qandahari's gory speech was nothing but a mere threat from *another Islamic fundamentalist.* But to me, it is a threat that must be taken seriously.

In the article, Abu Shihab Al-Qandahari said, *"… it is the only way to kill the maximum number of Americans… Eye for eye and tooth for tooth. If the Americans have bombs [referring to Nuclear Bombs] that no one else owns, Al-Qa`idah is stronger. It owns "dirty bombs" and "lethal virus bombs", which could cover the American cities with deadly* *diseases and turn this nation, which is "a professional in contempt for other nations," into a crowd of contaminated and sick people. The coming days would prove that Qa`idat al-Jihad is capable with Allah's help, of **turning the United States into a lake of lethal radiation,** that would seem as the last days of humanity…."*

Please understand that phrase *"…the last days of humanity…"* is indicative of the world coming to an end. And if you have any clue of what the Lord Jesus Christ has to say concerning *the last days,* not only will you know that *the end of this age* is near, you will also understand that the end will not come without a

▥▥▥▥ ✵ ▥▥▥▥

AL-QAEDA WANTS TO TURN THE UNITED STATES INTO A LAKE OF LETHAL RADIATION

precursor of some gruesome lethal thermonuclear fire, way beyond any man's imagination.

:: CLANDESTINE PRODUCTION OF NUCLEAR ARMS

Not many people are aware of the clandestine production and sales of nuclear weapons in the world. But the fact remains that the nuclear arms race is still going on strong. Nations like USA and Russia that believe they have the *"inherent right"* to own, sell, and profit from nuclear weapons are openly raking in billions of dollars, while those nations whom *the West* deems "*not to be trusted with nuclear weapons*" are busy acquiring them from the black-markets anyway. Nuclear weapons, regardless of the source, pose enormous danger to the human race. So any threat of nuclear attack from Al-Qaeda, Iran, or anyone else, no matter how remote, should be taken very seriously.

I assure you that the enemy's radar is on the United States of America right now. And those who do not believe that a nuclear weapon will be attempted on America sometime soon should think again because the enemy is armed to the teeth. I know this to be true the same way I knew that former President Bill Clinton would not be impeached from office when he went through his impeachment ordeal in 1998; the same way I knew that the Space Shuttle *Columbia* would crash and never rise again; and that President George W. Bush would be reelected in 2004. God reveals deep secrets to his servants before they happen.

As a *Seer* (1Samuel 9:9), I have the privilege of *seeing* some important events long before they happen. I knew all these to be true long before they ever became facts because I saw them ahead of time. A *Seer* speaks as a *Mouthpiece* of God and reveals the deep things of God as they are revealed to him from the very throne of God. As a *Seer*, I saw, ahead of time, that America would engage in a very divisive war, and thus become bombarded with all sorts of national and international conflicts at the peak of which *the enemy* will strike. Is America prepared for this attack?

:: AMERICA'S UNPREPAREDNESS

Is America prepared for another disaster of *9/11* or *Katrina* magnitude? I don't think so! With the general population still going about their business as usual; and with more terrorists sneaking into the country unnoticed, I suppose America is not ready for what I see coming. It is for this reason that the Lord compelled me to pray for the salvation of hundreds of millions of well-meaning Americans who go about their daily life trusting that their government will protect them.

The Lord also compelled me to intercede in prayers for the generality of American churches for their failure to take a stand and speak out on *hot issues* of national and international interests, even terrorism. Although many believers in Christ understand God's will for America, their general lackadaisical attitude towards major social, economic, and political issues have largely contributed to their powerlessness and diminished believability. Thus they are more like toothless bulldogs. With their watered-down messages, they bark, but they hardly bite the adversary.

The ripple effect of America's spiritual apathy is a continued moral degradation and downward spiral in the social, economic, and political arenas wherein more and more citizens fail to discern the difference between good and evil let alone recognize the signs of the times. Against this backdrop, I am now compelled to share with you what the Lord has revealed to me, that you may take responsibility for your own destiny before it is too late.

::CHAPTER FOUR

WHERE WE ARE NOW

For us to know where we are now and how we got here, let's take a quick look at some of the major terrorist acts perpetuated by Al-Qaeda and other terrorist networks in the last decade:

February 26, 1993:
Bombing of the World Trade Center
A powerful car bomb explodes in a garage underneath the World Trade Center in New York. Explosion kills six and wounded hundreds more.

June 25, 1996:
Bombing of U.S. Air Force Residence
Bomb kills 19 U.S. Air Force members at Khobar Towers a military housing development in Dhahran, Saudi Arabia.

August 7, 1998:
US Embassies Bombings
Simultaneous bombings at the U.S. embassies in Kenya and Tanzania, killing 224 people mostly Kenyans.

October 12, 2000:
Attack on USS Cole in Yemen
Bomb attack on the American Navy warship: *Destroyer USS Cole*, in Yemen, crippling the vessel, killing 17 sailors and injuring 39 others. 23 convicted Al-Qaeda terrorists responsible for the bombing escaped Feb. 3, 2006 from a Yemeni prison via a 140-meter long tunnel.

Sept. 11, 2001 (9/11):
World Trade Center Bombing

Al-Qaeda suicide hijackers crashed two jumbo jets into the World Trade Center in New York. The Twin Towers collapsed, killing almost 3,000 people. A third hijacked plane smashed into the Pentagon in Washington, and an attempt to ram a fourth plane [into the White House] failed after passengers forced the plane to crash land.

March 11, 2004:
Madrid Train Bombings

A series of coordinated terrorist bombings on the Madrid (Spain) commuter train system. The attacks killed 191 people and wounded 1,460.

September 1, 2004:
Beslan School Hostage Crisis

Terrorists attacked *the Beslan School* in Russia. The stand-off lasted three days. At the end, 344 people, of which 186 were children, were killed. Hundreds more wounded.

July 7, 2005:
The London Bombings

A series of coordinated suicide bombings that killed 52 and injured 700. Three of the bombs exploded on the London underground trains, and the fourth on a bus.

The War in Iraq

The war in Iraq remains the most divisive element in

America today. With the Middle East set ablaze and Iraq turned into a haven for terrorists, there is no man-made machinery that can stop the *madness* from prompting other wars. The land is filled with the blood of innocent people now crying out to God for justice. According to the United Nations, over 2 million Iraqis have already fled Iraq, while thousands have lost their lives, homes, families, and livelihood. But the anxiety is yet to hit the peak. With the British and Australian troops soon to be completely out of Iraq, and Iran not making things any easier for the U.S., the picture is not looking pretty.

On the homeland, things are not looking good either. The dividing line between America's lawmakers and the White House is widening up by the minute; and the bone of contention remains *the War in Iraq;* plus the Economy, Immigration issue, etc; the controversy continues to gather steam.

:: THE MANY FACES OF TERROR

For decades, evil has been rearing its ugly face in many aspects of life in America and the rest of the world. Unfortunately, it is not done yet. As evil is fast manifesting its ugly face in various facets of life in the Middle-East, a terror unprecedented is about to show up right here on the American soil. Regardless of our place of origin, career, economic status, race, gender, religious persuasion, or political preference, evil is our common enemy. While it shows up in one region as HIV/AIDS, it is poverty and hunger in another. Still in others, it is bombings and fear of nuclear attacks. Regardless of how evil manifests in your society, its purpose is to terrorize you.

The word "Terror" is associated with Fear. Fear induces torment. The word "Torment" is derived from the original Greek word "kola-sis" (kol'-as-is), meaning penal infliction or severe punishment (1John 4:18). To be tormented is to be inflicted with intense bodily pain and/or mental agony. The primary goal of terrorists is to bring about maximum bodily harm and severe mental agony.

January 2006:
Threatening the American people, Osama bin Laden, in his audiotape message, warns that Al-Qaeda's plans for the next terror attacks on the United States are under way. He is quoted as saying: **"...It's only a matter of time... they (the attacks) are in the planning stages, and you will see them in the heart of your land as soon as the planning is complete."**

Please understand that I neither patronize terrorists nor praise their "cause". It only seems to me that Al-Qaeda's promise is that its next rounds of attack on America will be deadlier than *9/11*. Little wonder why on February 2, 2006, US Defense Secretary Donald Rumsfeld (Retired) said, "...*the threat that we face today may be greater than ever before because the available weapons are far more dangerous...*" Think about it: what are the weapons now available to terrorists that Secretary Rumsfeld was referring to *"as far more dangerous."*

The Al-Qaeda that we face today is a regrouped and deadlier one. What makes the situation even more dangerous is the fact that Osama bin Laden is not alone in his mission to destroy America. There are many more powerful and influential persons, including persons in high government positions, who want to see America wiped out from the planet. I believe this to be true because, in a vision, the Lord revealed to me a *Trio,* among which was the ruling President of a certain country in possession of nuclear bomb. I assure that out there is a coalition deadlier than we all have imagined. The coalition is now set to destroy America beyond your wildest imagination. Now, how many nuclear bombs they have in their possession or have they the capacity to acquire remains a mystery. However, what is more important at this point is for the American people, and the whole world, to know for sure that the enemy has gained strength and access to nuclear weapons. And I assure you that unless the Lord supernaturally intervenes in the matter, America will soon become history.

Now that you have seen a clear picture of where we are, the question now remains as to where we are headed.

::CHAPTER FIVE

WHERE WE ARE HEADED

:: A NATION DIVIDED AGAINST ITSELF

In 2000, I saw a vision in which America was involved in a war. In the first scene, there were many helicopters and jets equipped with guns and bombs. However, the scene changed and I saw the nation involved in another war- a different kind of war; a war that prompted me to ask the question: "Why is America fighting against America?"

And afterward, there was so much panic in the land. And the Lord said to me "get hold of your passport". Immediately I ran to the room where my passport was, got hold of it, and came back out. Then the Spirit of the Lord took me up to a great height where I could see everything from above. From this vantage point, I saw "the four corners" of the world [not suggesting that the earth is flat]. With the Lord directing me, I went to the nations of the earth, one after the other, to rescue the people. I went swiftly, telling the people what is about to happen; and the people eagerly responded and gladly followed me because they knew I was telling the truth as it came from God Almighty. Then I woke up.

As we transitioned into the new millennium, the Lord began to define my purpose, mission, and destiny, even as it relates to my calling as a Prophet to the Nations and as an instrument of change and transformation in these End-Times. *Passport* here indicates the Holy Spirit and the Power he bestows. It is that Power that grants access, authority, and wisdom to a person called to fulfill the mandate of God. In this particular vision, there are three basic revelatory components:

- **First:** a first kind of war involving America; with heavy military weapons and artilleries including aircraft, missiles and others. This, I believe, is the current Iraq war.

- **Second:** another kind of war, which I believe is the current internal social, economic, and political conflicts and rancor now engulfing America. This was happening to the point that I asked why the nation was at war with itself.

- **Third:** Right before the inevitable, I was empowered by God (as many other willing/faithful believers will be) to bring forth a message of hope, relief, and deliverance not just to the American people but also to the four corners of the earth. This is the revival that many have prophesied- a revival that will storm America. But many do not know how it will begin or what will prompt it. Thus the Church must be well-prepared for this coming rush as millions of people will put their trust in the Lord and be saved. Thus we are beginning to see clear signs of desolations that will quicken the revival and cause the gospel of the kingdom to be preached in all the world for a witness unto all nations; and then shall the end come (Matthew 24:14).

:: AMERICA DIVIDED

On the international scene, America remains the most controversial figure especially with this awfully controversial war in Iraq. At home, the nation is at war against itself. And so the prophetic question as to why America is fighting against America points to the spiritual condition of a nation divided against itself; for a nation divided against itself cannot stand. Today, America is riddled with national and international controversies; divided over almost everything, including God.

EVERY KINGDOM DIVIDED AGAINST ITSELF WILL BE BROUGHT TO DESOLATION

The war in Iraq and everything associated with it has generated the rancor that has continued to undermine the fabric of the American society. Sadly, majority of Americans fail to see the handwriting on the wall. They fail to understand that a terror unprecedented is about to occur, and the Iraq war is antecedent to it. Though people are beginning to sense the perilous times in which we now live, some would rather take a "politically correct" position, contending that the crises plaguing the American society today are nothing but typical. The truth is America is now manifesting the characters of a spiritually fractured society. The social, economic, and political crises of today are signals of the spiritual flaw that will ultimately make way for the most feared external aggression of our time. The enemy understands that it is only a matter of time before the nation's protective wall cracks-open, and access granted; for a nation divided against itself cannot stand:

> **Matthew 12:25** ...*Every kingdom divided against itself is brought to desolation; and every city or house divided against itself shall not stand...*

> **Mark 3:24** *And if a kingdom be divided against itself, that kingdom cannot stand.*

I have the privilege of hearing from God and understanding the warning signals of these times. Part of the warning signals for this hour is the war in Iraq; a war that was revealed to me three years before it officially began in March 2003. Thus God has compelled me to bring you this revelatory message of freedom and deliverance.

:: REVELATION

Revelation is a divine enlightenment or understanding-*knowledge or information that you did not previously have.* God gives you a revelation to:

- *Tell you of things that will happen in the future.*
- *Confirm what you already sense that God is saying to you.*

- *Provide you with new direction for your life.*
- *Correct past mistakes, reconstruct the present, and build the future.*
- *Reveal conditions for change in your life, family, community, or nation.*
- *Provide divine perspectives, insights, and inspiration for specific situations.*
- *Release message of grace/mercy in your life, people, nation, or situations.*

God speaks and reveals information to man in several ways including:

- God's Audible Voice:
  1Samuel 3:10, Acts 9:3-7, Joshua 5:13-15
- God's Still Small Voice:
  1Kings 19:12
- Dreams:
  Genesis 15:1, 20:3, 28:12, 31:24, 37:5-10; Daniel 2; Matthew 1& 2
- Praying in the spirit:
  1Corinthians 14:5-6; 13-15; 26
- Word of Knowledge/Wisdom:
  John   5:19-20;   8:38-40,   Hebrews   5:14,
  1Corinthians 12:7-11
- Discernment:
  1Corinthians 12:7-11
- Illumination of Scripture (Hearing by the word of God): Romans 10:17

- Open Vision:
  Numbers 24:4-16, 1Samuel 3:1
- Night Vision:
  Job 20:8; 33:15, Isaiah 29:7, Micah 3:6, Daniel 2:19; 7:2, Acts 16:9; 18:9
- Prophecy:
  1Corinthians 12:7-11

God's will is for us all to receive wisdom by His Spirit so that we are not ignorant of His good and perfect will for our personal lives, communities, and nations:

> **Acts 2:17** *And it shall come to pass in the last days, saith God, I will pour out of my Spirit upon all flesh: and your sons and your daughters shall prophesy, and your young men shall see visions, and your old men shall dream dreams:*

True revelation is orchestrated by the Holy Spirit. Confirmed by the written Word of God, the purpose is to help us to see things God's way, and thus have godly perspectives. Against this backdrop, I will now share with you a number of revelations, some of which I have already shared with the White House. And while I acknowledge that some portions of this journal have been re-worded for clarity purpose only, I assure you that the record remains essentially the same.

::CHAPTER SIX

REVELATIONS ABOUT AMERICA

::THE WIND OF ADVERSITY HITS
(A NATION'S GLORY TURNS TO SHAME)

September 12, 2001 7:30 a.m. Atlanta:
I woke up around 4:30 am, and I read from the Bible the book of Ephesians chapters 5 & 6. Afterwards, I went back to sleep. *Then in a vision, by the Spirit of God, I saw a gigantic American flag towering in the sky. I perceived the flag to be as high as the twin towers. It was really beautiful and was held at both ends by a network of steel poles. Interestingly, this flag did not look like an ordinary flag made from cloth or canvass. It shone like glass and glittered under the sun. As I looked, I heard the Lord say,* **"Hold fast to your position because the wind is about to blow"**. *He also told me to carefully observe how the flag was going to be destroyed in a short time by a "thunderstorm". He instructed me to hold fast to my position, so I would not be affected by the devastation that was about to come. In an attempt to secure my position, I literally dug my feet in and held on tight to my pillow. Then it happened suddenly. Whatever it was, sounded like a combination of lightening, thunder, and a mighty rushing wind. It came in swiftly and tore up the flag and the steel poles came down. The flag was destroyed beyond recognition. The vibration shook everything, including my bed, but I held on tight. Then I woke up.*

As I spent time in the presence of the Lord, I discerned that the flag represented the glory of America, and that glory is about to turn to shame. For a nation that exalts itself against the knowledge of God runs a big risk of being destroyed by God. But this is not for America's enemies to glory in; it is for all of us to humble ourselves before God that He may lift us up in time of trouble.

THE WIND OF ADVERSITY IS ABOUT TO BLOW. IS AMERICA'S GLORY ABOUT TO TURN TO SHAME?

Now, because this vision specifically came to me one day after *9/11*, I knew for sure that God was not talking to me about what had already happened. He sure was talking about something that is yet to happen; something that seemed way bigger than *9/11*. So let us all be in prayers for America.

In the vision, I was instructed to hold fast to my position because *"the wind is about to blow"*. Consider this phrase and ask yourself if this is a wind of peace or that of adversity. Obviously it is a wind of adversity, destruction, and devastation. Consider what the scripture has to say about this:

> **Jeremiah 51:1** *Thus saith the LORD; Behold, I will raise up against Babylon, and against them that dwell in the midst of them that rise up against me, a destroying wind* (**spirit of a destroyer**).

The "wind" is indeed *the destroyer*. And according to this Bible prophecy, the destroyer is sent to destroy sinful Babylon and bring its glory to naught. Likewise, a "wind of adversity" is about to blow over *Babylon America*. Therefore, as a people, we ought to fear God and seek His mercy at this crucial time.

:: SPACE SHUTTLE COLUMBIA CRASHES

March 8, 2002, 4:30 a.m., Atlanta GA USA:

In this vision, I watched the Space Shuttle Columbia take off. It had a beautiful American flag attached to its tail end. It flew around for a while, displaying its beauty to the throngs of people watching. I was in the Spirit, and I stood there watching, amazed at the greatness of America. The Shuttle displayed its beauty for a little while and then received instruction to proceed with its journey. Then it went out of sight into outer space. At this stage, I felt the need to rest, so I proceeded in a certain direction towards my left, but the Holy Spirit stopped me immediately and instructed me to go towards my right where there was a Shelter (a building). [Please take note of the "left" and "right" directives]. I went into the building and laid down to rest. After a while, the Spirit of God told me to step back outside and take another look at the Shuttle in the sky. What I saw was a strange sight: the Shuttle was suspended in outer space for a moment, and then it tumbled down. I watched the Shuttle fall and hit the ground three times. The first time it hit the ground, a robotic helicopter-like device fell out from it. The second time it hit the ground, it was the food supply that was flung out. I saw a fish tossed out in my direction. The Shuttle hit the ground the third time and never rose again. Then a multitude of people began to walk toward the crash site. They asked me questions about what I had seen and heard. I narrated the prophetic dimension of what I had seen and I saw many other people (also with prophetic insights) bear witness to this truth. Then I awoke.

Today, the Shuttle Columbia is no more. The words "left" and "right" in this narrative are indicative of Spiritual directives:

"Left" is an indication of flesh or worldliness, and "Right" signifies Spirit or Righteousness.

Here, I was being instructed by the Holy Spirit to NOT lean on the strength and wisdom of man ("left") because they will inevitably fail. Instead, He instructed me to lean on the "right", which is the strength and wisdom of the Lord that can never fail [Matthew 25:33].

The same applies to you as you read this book. Do not dismiss my claim as coming from a mere man. Do not put your trust in religion, intellectualism, political correctness, wealth, or America's military might, for these will surely fail you in time of great need. Everything else will fail, but the Lord and His promises can never fail. Although the accident with the Shuttle happened almost a year after it was revealed to me, there is a dimension of this vision that points to a prophetic witness of the truth of God's word for the 21st Century believers. Not only will more and more Ministers of the Gospel of Jesus walk in greater revelation and understanding of the times, the time has also come when the nations of the world will literally storm the Church for answers/solutions to their misfortunes. Many people in the world marketplace are about to come to the shocking realization that they have been duped, and that many of their so-called democratic leaders have no real solutions to their nations' social, economic, and political woes. They will then have no other choice than to turn to Jesus Christ. And as the United States, Russia, China, Iran, and other nuclear powers and nuclear power aspirants openly gear up for a major nuclear showdown in this 21st Century, true members of the Body of Christ will also rise up to bear witness to the Will and Power of God– the Father of our Lord Jesus Christ, who saves those who put their trust in Him.

:: THE MUSHROOM CLOUD

June 2002, Atlanta GA USA:

In this vision, I saw two men dressed in military attire. I did not see their faces, I only saw their backside. Their nationalities were not revealed to me. I did not see the exact color of their uniform but I knew by the Spirit of God that they wore military attire. The background setting of the vision was such that there were many people around, for it *was a somewhat busy business arena. My focus was on these two men as my eyes followed them about. Then something strange happened: a **Woman** saw them carrying a bomb and shouted, "BOMB!". As her shout alerted everyone, the two men began to run toward the woman to stop her from giving them away. Realizing the urgency of the situation, I reached out and grabbed a bunch of people including my family, and we began to run for our lives. As we ran off, I looked back to see what was going on. And that was when I saw it- **a mushroom cloud**. Then I realized the unbelievable had happened. It was at that point that I screamed out from the depth of my spirit- "**Atomic Bomb!**" Then I woke up.*

Atomic bomb implies sudden destruction. (Acts 2:17, 19; 1 Thessalonians 5:3). As self explanatory as this vision is, there is one key element that I need to emphasize here:

The *Woman* who shouted *"Bomb!"*, is symbolic of the Church of Jesus Christ. These are the true apostolic and prophetic people who will perceive these things in the Spirit and try to announce it even before it happens. The point here is that the anti-Christ spirit, encompassed in religion, intellectualism, secularism, political correctness, and all kinds of societal façade, acting wickedly as always, will try to silence the Prophets, even the Church, not only through political maneuvering but also by sheer physical and religious pressure to keep the truth from being told. But those who know God shall be strong, and do *exploits* i.e. make the most of the privileged information given to them to save many lives and transform the world (Daniel 11:32-33)]. And they [the Prophets of the Lord) that understand (the signs of the times) among the people shall instruct, inform, and teach many people **(and Revival shall spring forth). And those who** refuse to listen/follow this instruction shall fall by the sword (war), and by flame (lethal fire/exploding bombs), by captivity (refugees), and by spoil (loss), *many days* according to Daniel 11:33.

January 18, 2003:
After delivering a speech on *Faith-Based Initiatives & Government Grants* at a church in Santa Rosa Beach, Florida, I had the privilege of sharing some of these visions with other associates of mine. That night, behind closed doors, we freely shared, and together we all prayed that God would forgive America and save His people from destruction. As I said earlier, many have also seen and heard from the Lord concerning these things but they are reluctant to share them publicly for fear of persecution for political and cultural *"incorrectness"*.

:: NUCLEAR ATTACK ON AMERICA

February 1, 2003, 5:52 a.m., Atlanta GA USA:
I was up till 2:30 am that particular night, but as soon as I got into bed, I felt an urge to pray. Because I did not immediately know what to pray about, I simply began

to pray in the Spirit [praying in tongues]. That night, my wife was spending the night at her sister's house, so I called her up to join me in prayer. We prayed together on the phone for about an hour or so. Afterwards, I went to bed. It was then I saw this vision:

I saw war, and many missile-launching fighter jets. And I saw America rise up to the task, destroying the enemy aircraft and other targets. Then I saw another war, deadlier than the first. This time it was in America. I saw many people running towards the **South.** *This war was much more intense than the first. I saw what appeared to be red-hot fire. There was much pandemonium, and people ran toward a safe place. This safe place was a large basement belonging to the Apostolic and Prophetic gathering called the Church.* **The place was highlighted as a place of refuge for everyone who chose to come.** *There was so much horror, and people were so fearful that some even attempted to run out from the place of refuge. But I and some others stood at the gate and ministered to the people, reassuring them that God's grace was sufficient.*

I found it peculiar that we had just enough time to help the people get to safety, away from the view of the enemy aircraft hovering all over the place. I remember telling the people that they would be shot at [by the hovering aircraft] if they left the place of refuge. I found it interesting that the enemy aircraft could not penetrate the place of refuge. I also noticed that anyone who stepped out of the safety provided by the place of refuge fell victim to the enemy aircraft. Somehow in this vision, I was also reminding the people that this war had been prophetically revealed to me long before it began, and I warned many people to take cover at the place of refuge because it was their only hope.

I woke up from the vision and prayed Psalm 91 over America. I was on my way to the office that particular afternoon of February 2, 2003 when I heard the tragic news of the crash of the *Shuttle Columbia.* Even though I wrote these visions down, it was not until the Space Shuttle had the accident that I began to pay more careful attention to them.

Applicable Scriptures include:

> **Psalm 64:7** *But God will shoot his arrow (**bomb, missile**) at them; they will be wounded suddenly.*

> **Proverbs 6:15-19** *Therefore calamity will come upon him **suddenly**; in a moment he will be broken beyond healing.*

> **Proverbs 29:1** *He who is often reproved [corrected], yet stiffens his neck [stubborn] will suddenly be broken [destroyed] beyond healing.*

The word **"South"** in the narrative does not necessarily indicate a geographical location or physical direction.

South, by the Holy Spirit, often indicates sin, corruption, deception, and worldliness:

> **Joshua 10:40** *So Joshua smote all the country of the hills, and of the South, and of the vale, and of the springs, and all their kings: he left none remaining, but utterly destroyed all that breathed, as the LORD God of Israel commanded.*

ROCKETS OR MISSILES SYMBOLIC OF SWIFT DESTRUCTION, SUDDEN OR UNEXPECTED ATTACK OR WAR.

One cannot continue to live in sin and expect the grace of God to abound (Romans 6:1). According to the word of God, sinful people and nations will be judged and devastated. I know that some will suggest that God, by His loving character and nature, cannot possibly do all these devastating things the Bible asserts. But I want to re-affirm that God is Love, and by character and nature, He is also a *Just* God. He has no choice but to judge our sins, even though, in His mercy, He does not even judge us as hard as our sins deserve (Psalm 103:10).

One thing I find quite amazing about the love of God is that, before the judgment of our sins and corruptions, God Himself provides us with a way of escape by announcing the impending judgment way ahead of time,

so as to give us an opportunity to repent and be forgiven. Therefore, the Lord is announcing this impending judgment on America ahead of its time so America can repent and be forgiven.

As you may have observed in the preceding narrative, God has provided America with a way of escape- *a place of refuge*. The "Place of Refuge", as it was called in the vision, is what the Bible calls "Cities of Refuge". Cities of refuge are established to provide protection and hope to a repentant sinner who sincerely recognizes his sin, admits his guilt, regrets his actions, asks for forgiveness, and seeks God's loving presence appropriately.

:: THE CITIES OF REFUGE

There were six cities of refuge enumerated in the Old Testament. They were all located on the hills *[indicative of the Church being referred to as a City on a Hill]* so that they will be easy to find by those seeking redemption/ protection. The Cities were meant for the redemption of sinners who sought refuge in the Lord. **Interestingly, the cities of refuge prophetically refer to Jesus Christ- the only true hope and refuge for mankind:**

> **Joshua 20:7** *And they appointed **Kadesh** in Galilee in mount Naphtali, and **Shechem** in mount Ephraim, and **Kirjatharba**, which is Hebron, in the mountain of Judah.*

Joshua 20:8 *And on the other side Jordan by Jericho eastward, they assigned* **Bezer** *in the wilderness upon the plain out of the tribe of* **Reuben***, and* **Ramoth** *in Gilead out of the tribe of Gad, and Golan in Bashan out of the tribe of Manasseh.*

Joshua 20:9 *These were the cities appointed for all the children of Israel, and for the stranger that sojourneth among them, that whosoever killeth* **any** *person at unawares might flee thither, and not die by the hand of the avenger of blood, until he stood before the people.*

Now let us consider these six Cities of Refuge:

- **Kedesh in Galilee in mount Naphtali.** Kedesh means Holiness: *Jesus, our righteousness.*

- **Shechem in mount Ephraim.** Shechem means Shoulder: *Upon Jesus' shoulder rests the government of God over the nations.*

- **Bezer in the wilderness upon the plain.** Bezer means Fortification: *Jesus, a protection to those who put their trust in Him.*

- **Kirjatharba, which is Hebron, in the mountain of Judah.** Kirjatharba means Fellowship: *Jesus, who restores us back into fellowship with God.*

- **Golan in Bashan.** Golan means Joy: *Jesus, in whom we are justified, though we sinned and fell short of the glory of God.*

- **Ramoth in Gilead.** Ramoth means High and Exalted: *Jesus, though sinless, was crucified like a criminal (for our sake). But God exalted Him and bestowed on Him the name, which is above every other name, government, political power, title, situation, or circumstance. That at the name of Jesus every knee must bow, in heaven and on earth and under the earth, and every tongue confess that Jesus Christ is Lord, to the glory of God the Father (Philippians 2:9-11).*

Thank God for America's arsenal, but I call on the American people, and the people of the world to put their trust not in the *false security* that physical arsenal alone provides. We all must put our whole-hearted trust in the name of the Lord (2 Chronicles 32:8). The arm of the flesh will fail you, but the Lord God is a high-tower and those who run to Him shall be safe from weapons of mass destruction.

Administration of the Cities of Refuge:

The administration and operations of the Cities of Refuge is not given to the politicians, lobbyists, intellectuals, scientists, psychics or philosophers of this world. It is the priests of God who are appointed to govern the affairs of the Cities of Refuge, which again points to the true Holy

Spirit-empowered members of the Body of Christ; not religious organizations or denominations. We appreciate the efforts of politicians, and men and women who labor daily for our benefit, and we thank God for their lives and contribution to humanity. But our confidence is not in the strength and wisdom of politicians, scientists, and bureaucrats. Our confidence is in the name of the Lord Jesus Christ.

References: Joshua 20:1-8, Proverbs 14:26, Isaiah 25:4, Philippians 2:9-11, Numbers 35: 10-15, Deuteronomy 19: 1-3.

::TERRORISTS ATTACK JETLINERS

February 13, 2003, 4:00 a.m., Atlanta GA USA:
I saw two regular civilian aircraft, probably 747s traveling in the air. Suddenly I saw two smaller civilian aircraft flying alongside these 747s. At first I thought they were all traveling in their respective directions, but then they came so close to one another. Then I realized that the second set of aircraft belonged to the enemy. One of the two enemy aircraft suddenly went for a head-on collision with the big civilian jetliner, but somehow it missed target in its first attempt. It came back again and this time around, it broke the wings of the big jetliner. I actually saw the wings of the jetliner fall off. This jetliner became distressed and began tumbling down to earth, and before long, it exploded into a ball of flames. Then the smaller aircraft, which looked more like a chopper, flew underneath the second civilian jetliner

*and collided with it from beneath, bringing complete destruction on the second jetliner. Then darkness fell upon the land. And I heard the loud voice of an angel of the Lord say, "I warned you ahead of time..." Then the **One** whose silhouette only I saw standing in front of me, and speaking to me in a very stern tone, said, "Did I not tell you to tell my Church to be ready with food and resources?" He then commanded me to tell the Church to prepare ahead of time. I trembled because the land was in total darkness.*

The word "Food" here is indicative of spiritual food, the true, unadulterated, Word of God. The word "resources" here indicates all kinds of material resources (including nutritious food, water, medical care, and other physical things/places required for *First Response during a time of disaster.* These are the things that a true City of Refuge (the true Church- the Body of Christ) must be able to provide to those who will come seeking refuge in the Lord, shelter from the storm, and cover from the wind of disaster that is about to hit America.

By this vision, I was commanded to tell the Church to be prepared to receive the mass of people who will come seeking refuge in the house of God when disaster does strike. I also felt a need for the U.S. Government to protect the airports and commercial airlines, and other places of significance. Thus I was prompted to tell the White House to pay more attention to the security situation at the Airports, and to position fighter jets to guard civilian jetliners. Thank God plain-clothed Air Marshals now accompany civilian flights.

:: SEVERE OIL/GAS SHORTAGE

February 14, 2003, 4: 00 a.m., Atlanta GA USA:
During my prayer time, a vision came to me by the Spirit of God: *I found myself in a gas station holding a gas pump on my left hand, and a napkin on my right. I held out the gas pump to the napkin and attempted to pump gas unto to the napkin. But instead of gas, only a few drops of water came out.*

Could this mean shortage of Gas? Will Gas prices go up? Is America about to experience severe shortage of Energy?

America is indeed experiencing shortage of gas and energy right now. According to a survey by the American Automobile Association, in the month of February 2003, regular unleaded gas prices averaged $1.663 a gallon in the United States. By the first week in June 2004, the nationwide average was well over $2.00. As of March 17, 2008, the average price was $3:20. Now where is America headed in terms of gas price- $5, $10, or $250 per gallon? Is the nation prepared for this kind of high level energy crisis?

The bottom-line of this particular vision is that there would be *Energy Shortage.* It was this vision that prompted me to suggest that America goes into a strategic partnership with some friendly Oil-producing nations, including Nigeria, to fill this need in time of emergency.

Should you be concerned about Oil/Gas scarcity? We all should be concerned about possible shortage of Oil/Gas because we are presently living on borrowed time. Tight global supplies, geopolitical uncertainties, and increasing demand were the primary elements generally pushing up the price of gasoline. But now other elements such as *Terrorism* are also directly affecting Oil and Gas supply:

February 7, 2006:
Exxon Mobil Senior Vice President, Stuart McGill, said the United States will always rely on foreign imports of Oil to feed its energy needs. Referring to what he called **the "mis-perception" that the United States can achieve energy independence**, Mr. McGill said that it is simply not feasible in any time period relevant to our discussion today to become energy independent. His comments came days after President Bush promised to help America "kick its addiction to Middle Eastern Oil".

Apart from Natural Disasters, which are bound to increase with Global Warming, there is also the war in Iraq, coupled with growing instability in the Middle East. With persistent anti-American sentiment in the Oil Producing nations, there is enough reason to be concerned. There is an ever-increasing demand for Oil/Gas especially in

America, China and India. America currently consumes 21 million barrels daily- *a quarter of world supply.*

Today, the Oil Industry is more threatened than it has ever been in decades. Between 2003 and 2006, there were intermittent terror attacks on the Oil Industry. Right now all eyes are on the following nations:

- *Saudi Arabia, as suicide bombers stormed the world's biggest oil processing plant (Feb. 2006);*
- *Nigeria, as militants kidnapped four foreign oil workers but released them after 19 days (Jan. 2006);*
- *Iraq, as insurgents blow up pipelines from the country's northern fields, halting the flow of oil to Turkey terminals for shipment abroad (Jan. 2006).*
- *Many more adverse things have happened since 2006 up till now.*

You should be concerned because a major and prolonged scarcity of Oil in America will lead to unbearable situations like shutting down of Schools, closing of Postal Services, grounding of Transportation systems, and closure of production Companies. As you pray that winter never comes, food prices will skyrocket and the economy may simply grind to a halt. And what will happen to other sectors of the economy including Real Estate? Listen to the experts: In 2006, Susan M. Wachter, professor of real estate at the Wharton School of the University of Pennsylvania asserted that anything that causes the economy to go into recession will cause the real estate market to go-under. Now you know why we all should be genuinely concerned about shortage of Oil and Gas.

:: TERRORIST NATION AGAINST AMERICA

February 16, 2003, 4: 00 a.m., Atlanta GA USA:
I woke up to meet with the Lord. Before I went back to sleep, I asked the Lord for a Word concerning these visions about the future of America. As I continued in prayer, I heard (by the Spirit of God) a loud voice say, *"A Sword has been driven to the ground" even as I saw a Sword come from heaven and strike the soil of America. I realized that a Sword has been drawn against America.*

Prophetically, "Sword" implies War. The Sword is an instrument of war against whom it is drawn. With a sword striking the land, I believe that an important decision concerning America has been made in Heaven. I suppose there will be war right here on the soil of America. This will be a different kind of war. Compared to the Iraq war, this war will be of greater magnitude and dimension. I feel compelled to refer you to the book of Ezekiel the 21st chapter concerning the *swind- an instrument of terror that God raised up against His beloved Israel.* This instrument of terror translated into a "terror" or "rogue" nation that the Lord used to punish Israel when Israel rebelled against the Lord. With the sword out of its sheath, the fate of the nation was sealed, and the judgement and awful wrath of God was decreed to come upon Israel. God allowing a terrorist nation to war against Israel and prevail, as a punishment for Israel's rebellion, gives us a tremendous insight to this unique way by which the Lord would punish rebellious nations even in today's world.

> **Ezekiel 21:1-5** *And the word of the LORD came unto me [Ezekiel the prophet of the Lord], saying, Son of man, set thy face toward Jerusalem, and drop thy word toward the holy places, and prophesy against the land of Israel, And say to the land of Israel, Thus saith the LORD; Behold, I am against thee, and will draw forth my sword out of his sheath, and will cut off from thee the righteous and the wicked. Seeing then that I will cut off from thee the righteous and the wicked, therefore shall my sword go forth out of his sheath against all flesh from the south to the north: that all flesh may know that I the LORD have drawn forth my sword out of his sheath: it shall not return any more.*

:: THE SIEGE MOUNTS

August 2003, Atlanta GA USA:
In another night vision, I saw five enemy fighter jets fly quietly from overseas into the United States. Nobody seemed to notice them as they came silently and landed in the woods; but I kept my eyes on them. I heard the Lord say "they are from Germany". Then I saw the five spies come out of the

woods in civilian clothing. Afterward I lost sight of them because they blended-in with the crowd. Then I woke up.

Probably unknown to the general public, the siege against America is now mounting. I suppose that enemy operatives and terrorist sleeper cells are being positioned, awaiting further instructions. I believe that this is what is being revealed to me; and we must take the message very seriously.

What about the Germany Connection? *I believe that majority of the Islamic terrorists are being armed with the spirit and mindset of the murderer Adolf Hitler. You would recall that Adolf Hitler was the one who masterminded the Holocaust. Now these Islamic radicals have masterminded a plan to perpetuate a nuclear Holocaust in America.*

October 2005:
President Ahmadinejad of Iran sparked widespread international criticism when he called for Israel to be wiped off the map. Calling the Holocaust a myth, President Ahmadinejad also denies the killing of six million Jews by the Nazis. Well, right about the same period that President Ahmadinejad made this awful statement, I saw a vision in which the Spirit of the Lord took me (in a moment of time) to see the reality of the Holocaust by showing me the Nazi's Death Chambers. And so to someone like me, the Holocaust is not a myth; it is a reality: a matter that touches the very heart of God. It is one thing to

stand up against American policies in the Middle-East; but it is another thing to advocate complete destruction of God's people from the face of the earth. I believe that the spirit of the Nazis' Adolf Hitler is now operating in the Middle-East, inciting terrorists to perpetuate a nuclear holocaust not just in Israel, but also in the United States of America.

IIIIIII ⊛ IIIIIII

MAKE NO MISTAKE ABOUT IT, WAR HAS BEEN DECLARED ON AMERICA

:: NUCLEAR BOMB ACTIVATED (CLOCK BEGINS TO TICK)

February 5, 2004, 2:45 a.m., Atlanta, GA USA: *In a vision, by the Spirit of the Lord, I saw three people from a distance. One of them was revealed to me as the current President of a nation, but the name of the nation was withheld. He was undoubtedly the leader of the trio. Although this President posed as a civilian President, he sure had the posture of a military President. The other two individuals appeared more like civilians. The three of them entered into a pact in a secret warehouse-like building that I later realized was a secret laboratory. It appears like the mystery President was supplying the two civilians with the nuclear Bomb. The three of them nodded in agreement to activate the nuclear bomb. It was as if they needed each other's approval or consent. One after the other, each of them did what* he was supposed to do to approve. The President was the last to act. It was as if he (the mystery President) joined together the ends of two electric cords; for as soon as he did, I heard a "click" sound, and **the bomb was activated. I saw the clock begin to tick. At that, I was alarmed, for it meant that the bomb will soon go off.** Afterward they came out of the building. A small bomb, probably a grenade, was then thrown at the building [by one of the guards who were with them]. The grenade-like bomb was thrown at the doors to seal the doors of the Lab so that no one could ever go in or come out of that building again. The small bomb killed the five or six scientists who worked in the laboratory so they would not be alive to tell any tales.

The vision was so vivid that even the sparks from the explosion came very close to the door where I stood; and I had to duck instinctively to avoid being scorched by the sparks. As soon as it dawned on me that the **activated nuclear bomb** was directed at America, I began to cry. Looking up to Heaven, I cried out loud to God the Father, and reminded Him of His promise to keep me safe and to accomplish His destiny for my life. Immediately, God spoke to me and reassured me that He would keep me safe and fulfill His will for my life. Then I woke up.

I woke up knowing that the enemy already has the bomb. The deal has been struck; the bomb has been made available or it definitely will be made available to the enemy. It is only a matter of time before it happens. It seemed to me that the fate of this great nation has been sealed. Whoever this mysterious President is, it is obvious to me that he has access to nuclear bombs, and can produce, give, or sell at will to these two civilian blood-mongers.

I narrated the vision to my wife and other intercessors; and we all prayed for God to forgive and save America from destruction.

According to this vision, this mystery President has aligned with two individuals with the intent to destroy America. In the whole wide world, there are only four key public figures that have publicly declared their desire to wipe-out America and Israel from the face of the earth. Apart from Osama Bin Laden and Al Zawahiri, President Mahmoud Ahmadinejad of Iran and his supreme leader the Grand Ayatollah Ali Khamenei are two other public figures, who have publicly acknowledged their unparalleled hatred for Israel and America.

Pertaining to this mysterious President, some associates of mine have suggested such names as Pyongyang of North Korea or Hu Jintao of China. But I see someone else; someone much more powerful, more determined, and more influential. I see Russia's President Vladimir Putin, a high-ranking "former" KGB officer who is currently consolidating social, economic, and political power with a mission to restore Russia's lost glory. With Putin in the picture, it is not difficult to imagine that Iran, somehow, has managed to acquire one of the Old Soviet Union's "inadequately secured" atomic bombs, and the bomb may someday be used against the U.S. If we couple this with the fact that Russia is the main contractor building Iran's nuclear facility, there is little surprise, therefore, that Mr. Putin is strongly opposed to the move by UN Security Council to impose economic sanctions on Iran for President Ahmadinejad's refusal to dismantle Iran's nuclear program. I know that right now all eyes are on Iran's President Ahmadinejad for his irate public speeches against Israel and America. Thus the West is trying to pile political and economic sanctions to prevent Iran from going ahead with its nuclear program.

Another interesting person to consider here is Pakistan's President, General Pervez Musharraf who signed a peace deal in 2006 with Pro-Taliban Militants. President Musharraf had faced heated allegations that Taliban forces in Afghanistan are receiving support and shelter from inside Pakistan, and that Pakistan's bizarre deal would reduce pressure on Al-Qaeda top figures, including Osama bin Laden, who is believed to be hiding in the region.

But whosoever this mysterious President is, he appears to me as a staunch adversary whose "destiny" is to facilitate the acquisition and the ultimate use of the atomic bomb against the United States. My strong feeling is that the mystery President and the two civilian terrorists, whoever they are, already have the bomb; and is only a matter of time before they use it. On the one hand, I sense that they are waiting for the right moment, possibly with a little provocation from the U.S. or Israel. Their intent is to destroy lives, cause a major economic collapse, and bring about the end of the American era. On the other hand, I sense that the Lord has held them back for now because the Church in America is not prepared for a major shock as this one is likely to be. The question is, what are you going to do if indeed the adversary succeeds in using a nuclear bomb against the U.S.?

My heart goes out to the general public: the everyday people- the common folks, who have no private jets by which they can fly out of the country in a short notice, and who have no ways and means to acquire anti-radiation devices or build multi-million dollar bunkers to hide in time of trouble. And yet majority of the American people seem to have no clue of the magnitude of what is about to hit them. However, I assure you that true refuge comes only from the Lord. The Lord will surely protect and preserve His own.

:: NUCLEAR ATTACK /MUSHROOM CLOUD

June 18, 2004, 5:45 p.m., Atlanta, GA USA:
In spite of the noise/activities in my family lounge, I fell into a deep sleep for a few minutes. Within those minutes (by the Spirit of the Lord) I saw myself outside of the building looking up in the sky. What I saw was a thick

cloud, more like a gigantic mushroom of smoke and dust fast covering the entire atmosphere. Then I heard the sounds of fighter jets roaring in the sky followed by explosions of all sorts. Then I awoke. I am reminded of God's word in the second chapter Joel:

> **Joel 2:30-32** *And I will show wonders in the heavens and in the earth, blood, and fire, and pillars of smoke. The sun shall be turned into darkness, and the moon into blood, before the great and the terrible day of the LORD come. And it shall come to pass, that whosoever shall call on the name of the LORD shall be delivered: for in mount Zion (the Church) and in Jerusalem shall be deliverance, as the LORD hath said, and in the remnant whom the LORD shall call.*

With thick clouds of smoke covering the atmosphere, and without electricity, darkness will engulf the land. But God remains a shinning Light to His people. In the midst of the darkness and confusion, God will continue to shine the light of His Power, Plan and Purpose on His Children through dreams, and visions, and prophecies:

> **Joel 2:28-30** *And it shall come to pass afterward, that I will pour out my spirit upon all flesh; and your sons and your daughters shall prophesy, your old men shall dream dreams, your young men shall see visions: And also upon the servants (males) and upon the handmaids (females) in those days will I pour out my spirit. And*

I will shew wonders (signs) in the heavens and in the earth, blood, and fire, and pillars of smoke.

My dreams and visions are actually consequent upon my in-filling with the Holy Spirit and baptism by *Fire*. The Scriptures Acts 2 and Joel 2 are essentially fulfilled in my life. And God is no respecter of persons: if He did it for me, He can do it for you. You are not supposed to be in the dark, and be caught unawares by a looming tragedy. The Church is supposed to be a light to a world in darkness. Unfortunately many a dead churches (asleep in the spirit by their false doctrines and abominable practices) constitute pathways of death to a world desperately in need of a Savior.

But the End-Times Scriptures will be fulfilled, whether you believe or not. You can believe, and be saved, and be guided by the same Holy Spirit who guides me. I do not practice yoga, witchcraft, psychics, chanting, false meditations, or any of those abominable practices; and I don't have dreams and visions at will. These things are revealed to me by the Holy Spirit.

My wife and children are also filled with Spirit of God. They also have dreams and see visions. Lately my wife has been having dreams and visions that further point to the need for us to pray for America. In 2006, she saw a vision in which cities were being engulfed by flood waters (possibly tsunamis). I do know that floods are signs of judgment of sin. Thus the sins of many regions will be judged with floods, hurricanes, tornadoes, etc. She also saw a vision of a large black fish lurking around the shores of America. This is probably an indication of enemy war-ship or a nuclear submarine. The following information corroborates this claim:

February 2007:

NewsMax Magazine reports that **in the fall of 2006,** a Chinese submarine surfaced in the Pacific Ocean just five miles away from the *USS Kitty Hawk* aircraft carrier. Interestingly, the Submarine came that close undetected. Worthy of note is the fact that China operates a massive impenetrable underground command center in Beijing.

Mount St. Helen:

I saw yet another vision in which the Mount St. Helen, a volcanic mountain in Washington State, was revealed to me. *In the spirit, I was elevated to the top of the Mount St. Helen. I was so close to it that I thought the volcano was going to erupt in my face, but instead, it caused such a severe earthquake that shook the entire region. Then I woke up.*

To understand these spiritual signposts, you have to look to God's wisdom in the scriptures:

> **Psalm 11:6** *On the **wicked** he will rain **coals of fire and brimstone; a scorching wind** shall be the portion of their cup.*

Scorching wind means destructive/devastating storms, hurricanes, and tornadoes. **Coals of fire and brimstone** refer to volcanic eruption and earthquake. While there will be more and more volcanic earthquakes that may even trigger tsunamis, what the Lord is also saying here is that there will be a government shake-up in Washington for their immorality, greed, corruption, and utter disregard for righteousness.

I also saw the Hand of the Lord remove the top of the Capitol, that the misdeeds of the Legislators may be exposed. This implies that many atrocities of the government and misdeeds of the Legislators will be exposed to the American people. Obviously this uncovering has already begun. The shake-up is already on in Washington. Cases of bribery and corruption are being exposed. Unprecedented lobbying, ear-marks, and money laundering are being uncovered. The sex-rings, cover-ups, as well as many other excesses are presently being exposed. But these expositions are not necessarily for you and me to rejoice over. It is for us all to recognize our frailty as human beings, fear the Lord who knows all secrets, and come to terms with our desperate need of Him not only in our very private lives, but also in our corporate social, economic, and political life. It is also a prime signal pointing to the fact **all things** (life, government, wealth, power, people, places, etc) are now tapering to an end-point in submission to God's Power, Plan, and Purpose for His creation (Acts 3:21).

:: SPIES PENETRATE AMERICA

January 1, 2006, 7:45 p.m., Atlanta, GA USA:
My whole family and a couple of guests joined us in celebrating the New Year. I had a short rest somewhat around six in the evening. I woke up an hour and forty-five minutes later with this vision vivid in my mind:

*I stepped outside of the house for a moment. I looked up and I noticed that the cloud above me was shaped into the outline an airplane. An airplane-shaped cloud will indeed catch anybody's attention. So I looked more closely, and yes, it was indeed the clouds shaped into an airplane. However-er, as I kept on looking, I noticed that the airplane-shaped cloud began to manifest into a real airplane. That caught my attention even the more; so I kept on looking. Then I saw five parachutes drop from the airplane. And the Spirit of the Lord said to me, "**Spies**". At that word I was alarmed, realizing that these were not just roadside terrorists but pro-fessional government spies sneaking into America, awaiting further instruction from their superiors. I ran back into the house to get my family to a place of safety. Then I woke up.*

The airplane-shaped cloud manifesting into a real air-plane is an indication of a **Camouflage**. I believe this revelation points more to a particular country that cur-rently maintains diplomatic relations with America. *Pro-fessional secret service operatives* of foreign governments sneaking into America unnoticed further corroborates my belief that some top-secret high-ranking military operatives of a particular enemy country are very much involved in the plot to sell, acquire, and use a nuclear bomb to devastate America. The question again remains as to who this mystery President is?

:: INTERCONTINENTAL BALLISTIC MISSILES (ICBM)

April 2006:

In a dream, the Spirit of the Lord took me far above the sky where I saw a mysterious aircraft. It was a Jet-Bomber carrying four (4) rocket-propelled Missiles. The interesting thing about this missile-carrying aircraft was that it went up high and flew far above the cloud before launching its weapons. I do not know for sure if this idea of flying far above the clouds has to do with radar-evasion or not, but I did see the clouds significantly far below the aircraft. Then with unmatched precision, the aircraft released the four missiles, one after the other, in a timed succession. I also noticed that each missile was capable of moving farther out (maneuvering) to hit its target without a hitch, implying that the missiles are designed to hit specific targets without fail.

I believe the Lord was revealing to me the formidable Intercontinental Ballistic Missile (ICBM) equipped with multiple independent nuclear warheads. The bomber "flying far up in the sky above the clouds" is indicative of Sub-Orbit Missiles traveling inter-continental, using sophisticated systems of navigation that allow the warheads to hit different targets thousands of miles away.

Wednesday May 30, 2007:
The Guardian reported that Russia has successfully tested a new **multiple-warhead intercontinental ballistic missile** capable of penetrating American defenses. The report also said that Russia's new RS-24 missile is capable of:

- *Carrying multiple independent warheads, making it almost impossible to shoot down by any existing defense systems.*
- *Using sophisticated systems of navigation, which allows each warhead to independently lock on to different targets.*
- *Traveling intercontinental to hit targets thousands of miles away.*

Although I saw this ICBM *vision* in April 2006, I did not take any particular interest in ICBMs until June 2007 when the G-8 met in Germany. This time, my attention was particularly drawn to ICBM by a vision revealed to me on the first day of the 2007 G-8 Summit. In the vision, *I saw one of Russia's ICBM penetrate America's airspace. In the vision, it actually flew over my head as it entered into America's airspace.*

The fact is, Russia now has these missiles that can easily penetrate the American defense. I know I cannot answer the question of who will launch an ICBM against America; whether Russia or its allies, I do not know. But one thing is for sure, the expertise to make and launch the ICBM that I saw in this vision came from Russia.

Russia's formidable ICBMs will conveniently hit any target in America if fired from Iran. You need to know that Russia is in a serious economic and diplomatic tie with Iran, and is already training Iran's military on the use of these sophisticated weapons. This implies that Iran can either acquire Russia's finished ICBMs or acquire the technology to make them. Other Middle-Eastern nations including United Arab Emirates and Syria are also adding Russian-made ICBMs to their arsenals.

:: BUSH'S ANTI-MISSILE DEFENSE

President Bush's proposal to build anti-Missile Defense Base at the backyard of Russia (in Poland and Czech Republic) is to reduce the threats posed by ICBMs from Iran and other nations in the Middle East. As you can imagine, Russia is vehemently opposed to the proposal. Today, some 19 countries have Ballistic Missile capabilities; 8 of them with nuclear weapons, and many others probably on the way.

The world believes that Iran and North Korea are on the verge of officially having nuclear-tipped ICBMs. While I recognize the obvious threats posed by Iran and North

Korea, I assure you that in the long run, America, China and Russia are themselves greater threats to the world where their nuclear arsenals are concerned. These nations are expending billions of dollars to amass Nukes that can practically destroy the world 10 times over:

Monday July 9, 2007:
According to Investors Business Daily Newspaper (Issues & Insights), Russia and China are currently building Nukes that will incinerate America in the event of war. Russia's Topol Missile (range 6,500 miles) is aimed directly at the U.S. China's CSSX-10 Missile with a range of 8,500 miles will conveniently strike America's West Coast. Truly, America does have adversaries; and America does need Christ desperately.

Perhaps you consider them silly these things I am saying, and you are wondering why you and/or your government should care about them. To some, all that I have been saying may be a lot of hot air, but not so to those privileged with the eyes to see and ears to hear the deep truth of God. Christ is the Creator of all things, powers, and authorities. He is the Lord over all nations. All things were created by Him and for Him. In Him everything exists, and all things have their being (Colossians 2). He knows all things- nothing is hidden from Him.

By His Providence, He reveals important information that men, in their very best intellect, strength, or ingenuity can never fathom. It is by Jesus Christ that I have seen and heard all these things, so that you may believe that He is the Lord who can save you from the wrath to come. He is sovereign over all things, even terrorism. He knows all events from the beginning to end, and He has them under His control; so much so that He can make all things work out well for the good of those who love Him; and turn bad things, even terrorism, into punishment for those who despise Him.

Those who allow Christ to rule and reign in their lives are the true Children of God. They are not Children of God because they are religious. They are Children of God because Christ redeemed them (by His Blood) from this world of sin, iniquities, and death. Prior to their redemption, they were Muslims (like I was), Hindus, Atheists, etc. None of them, absolutely none of them, was a child of God by right, birth, tradition, custom, or nationality. All were converted because they personally confessed the name of Jesus. *They used to be of the kingdoms of this world, but Christ redeemed them unto God, one life at a time, to be a Kingdom of Priests to rule and reign in the World (Revelation 5:10). Empowered by the Holy Spirit, their primary mission is to recover all things- social, economic, political, etc from the kingdom of darkness.*

As priests of God in government, business, and others arenas of life, they are to bring the Kingdom of Light to bear over the kingdom of darkness- casting out devils and overthrowing the powers of darkness in order to make the world a better place for us all. Equipped with privileged information and the uncommon wisdom of God, they are to influence life in governments, businesses, and communities the world over, establishing God's Government in their various circles of influence and aspects of life. For example Elisha was the Seer through whom God exposed the War Strategies of Syria- a staunch enemy of Israel. Listen to this interesting conversation between the king of Syria and his cabinet members:

> **2Kings 6:8-12** *Once when the king of Syria (Israel's enemy) was warring against Israel, he took counsel with his servants, saying, "At such and such a place shall be my camp." But the man of God (Prophet Elisha) sent word to the king of Israel, "Beware that you do not pass this place, for the Syrians are going down there." And the king of Israel sent to the place of which the man of God (Prophet Elisha) told him. Thus he used to warn him (king of Israel), so that he saved himself there more than once or twice. And the mind of the king of Syria was greatly troubled because of this thing; and he called his servants and said to them, "Will you not show me who of us is for the king of Israel?" And one of his servants said, "None, my lord, O king; but Elisha, the prophet who is in Israel, tells the king of Israel the words that you speak in your bedchamber (in secret).*

Like Elisha, I enjoy the privilege of seeing and hearing deep secret conversations that can help expose the plans of terrorists and literally turn a nation's fate around. Like the Prophet Elisha (2 Kings 6), I (and many others) are also called to righteously influence the social, economic, and political aspects of life in the nations in these End-Times. Like Elisha was prompted to relay these secrets to the king of Israel, I was also prompted to send a message to the king of America, in this case President Bush. Now I am compelled to speak directly to the American people through the pages of this book, that the people may see what I see and hear what I hear; and return to God. And hopefully avert these looming disasters.

::CHAPTER SEVEN

GOD'S PROVIDENCE

According to Webster's Collegiate Dictionary 10th Edition, Providence is God conceived as the power sustaining and guiding human destiny. **God's Providence, the Kingdom of God, or the Government of God covers the entire universe:** this includes all things both in the heavens, in the earth, and under the earth; natural and spiritual, including the affairs of men- both good and sinful. God cannot do evil and evil cannot do God. By His providence, God has the power to limit, restrain, allow, or turn evil around for the good of His children.

Regarding sinful actions of men, The **Web Bible Encyclopedia** *represent them as occurring by God's permission (Genesis 45:5; 50:20., 1Samuel 6:6; Exodus 7:13; 14:17; Acts 2:3; 3:18; 4:27, 28); and as controlled (Psalm 76:10) and overruled for good (Genesis 50:20; Acts 3:13). God does not cause or approve of sin, but He has the Power to limit, restrain, and overrule it for good.*

The Bible Encyclopedia goes on to say that the mode of God's providential government is altogether unexplained. It asserts the fact that God does govern all his creatures and all their actions; and that His **government is universal** (Psalm 103:17-19), particular (Matthew 10:29-31), efficacious (Psalm 33:11; Job 23:13), embraces events apparently contingent (Proverbs 16:9, 33; 19:21; 21:1), consistent with God (2Timothy 2:13); to His glory (Romans 9:17; 11:36).

Psalm 47 says God is the King of all the Earth; a Holy God who reigns over the heathen (a person, people, or nation that does not acknowledge/worship the God of the Bible). God's Holiness and Lordship over the Earth is explained by His providence to allow the sinful action of one nation (a heathen nation) as a punishment for the sinful action of a nation that does acknowledge/worship Him, without Him aiding or abetting the sins of either of them. God's decision to allow the sinful deeds of evil/idolatrous **Babylonia** as a punishment for the sin of His beloved Judah clearly explains this point. Like in every situation, God neither aided Judah's sins nor abetted Babylonia's evil; He punished both nations for their sins. Babylonia, in the Hand of God was therefore a *Sword* of punishment for sinful Judah.

:: BABYLON: A SWORD AGAINST JUDAH

According to the Biblical account in Ezekiel 21, the prophet Ezekiel foresaw Babylon's king Nebuchadnezzar's onslaught as *the Sword* that God would use to punish the misdeeds of rebellious Judah. Remember, Babylonia was a pagan nation, yet it would be God's "Sword" raised against Judah. Interestingly, the prophecy was so clear that it even foresaw king Nebuchadnezzar locating Judah by **divination**. This happened because the Lord had given Judah into the hands of its enemy for its open rebellion against the Lord. Essentially, Judah had become **spiritually fractured and internally weakened**, having despised its heritage and given itself to abominations and sins of idolatry. God then despised the nation in return and gave the people up to the reward of their wickedness. Today, many nations, including America, have become so familiar with God and blessings that they now take God for granted. It is one thing to sin against God; it is another thing to flaunt your sin before Him. To flaunt your sin before the Lord is to make Him remember all your sins, including those of your forefathers, and then punish you for them all:

> **Ezekiel 21:24** *Therefore thus says the Lord GOD: Because you have made your guilt to be remembered, in that your transgressions are uncovered, so that in all your doings your sins appear- because you have come to remembrance, you shall be taken in them.*

:: BABYLON YESTERDAY, IRAQ TODAY

God is sovereign over all the nations of the earth and He may choose whatever instrument He deems fit in executing swift judgment over any arrogant, atrocious, and idolatrous nation. Isn't it amazing that the people perpetuating all kinds of terrorist attacks in many nations today are mostly from the areas of ancient Babylon (now Iraq), Persia (now Iran), Assyria (now Syria), and other surrounding nations whose religion, Islam, stem from divination and the occult practices of ancient Babylonians? Is this making sense to you now?

:: PURPOSE OF ISRAEL IN THE EARTH

God raised up Israel to be a true example of a righteous nation. He then made a Covenant with the people and empowered them to be His instrument to disinherit sinful and idolatrous nations in the world, to overthrow their idols, and to restore righteousness in His earth. But somewhere along the line, Israel chose to cohabitate with the very idols and abominations it was called to destroy and eliminate from the face of the earth. Thus they broke Covenant with God. This was an *affront against God.* Therefore the anger of the Lord was kindled against Israel. In part, this is the root-cause of the trouble Israel is having with its surrounding Arab nations today. The Lord made those nations to be **a thorn** in the flesh of Israel- *a sore against Israel's peaceful settlement:*

> **Judges 2:1-3** *Now the angel of the LORD went up from Gilgal to Bochim. And he said, "I brought you up from Egypt, and brought you into the land which I swore to give to your fathers. I said, 'I will never break my covenant with you, and you shall make no covenant with the inhabitants of this land; you shall break down their altars.' But you have not obeyed my command. What is this you have done? So now I say, I will not drive them out before you; but they shall become adversaries to you, and their gods shall be a snare to you.*

:: AMERICA MUST LEARN FROM ISRAEL

Due to the nation's *affront against God*, I perceive that God, in His providence, may soon bring about a godly sorrow and repentance in America even by the sinful actions of terrorists (2 Corinthians 7:10). God will not change His mind without us rendering our sincere repentance, prayers, and petitions before the Lord. America must understand that God always has ready instrument to discipline those who rebel against Him.

Just like Israel, I believe America was raised up by God to be a *city upon the hill*- a place of refuge for those who truly desire freedom and liberty to live out their full potential in Christ Jesus. But today America has openly despised that calling by cohabitating with all manner of sinful lifestyles and abominations. The nation has openly despised God, and made His covenant of no effect. Worse still, America finds a way to legitimize many sinful and abominable lifestyles, justifying them by false doctrines of *love, freedom, and religious liberty*. Thus *the Land of the free* has now become *the land of the bound*. The claim that America was not established by God as a Christian nation is ignorant and pathetic. What a privilege and honor it is for a people to be set apart by God for exploits.

Unfortunately, after America became very prosperous, it forsook this great and high calling, and went a whoring after other gods. God loves America, but the nation is about to reap the consequences of *flaunting idolatry, throwing out the Ten Commandments from public places and banning prayers in public schools; legalizing abortion, legitimizing blasphemy, promoting pornography, and legitimizing homosexuality.* A sin will remain a sin no matter how much you legalize it. Legalizing a sin will not make it a virtue. No matter how hard we try to legalize it, a sin will always be a sin, abhorred by the Holy God.

As you prepare to read the next chapter, let me remind you that American legislators and judges successfully used corrupt politicking to cause the last two or three generations of parents and children to grow up without the word of God spoken in their schools. Now everyone is complaining about societal atrocities, immoralities, and home-grown terrorism. Let me quickly remind you of what God is saying to America now:

> **Hosea 4:6** *My people are destroyed for lack of knowledge: because thou hast rejected knowledge, I will also reject thee, that thou shalt be no priest to me: seeing thou hast forgotten the law of thy God, I will also forget thy children.*

The general lack of God's knowledge in the American society is not due to the absence of God's word. It is due to the sheer rejection of God's word by the high and powerful business men/women, scientists and philosophers,

bureaucrats and government officials all backed by corrupt lobbyists who will buy any government at any price
for their own selfish ends.

::CHAPTER EIGHT

SIN AND TERRORISM

God is Holy. He cannot cohabitate with sin as it runs contrary to righteousness and justice- *the foundation of His throne.* Although God loves us unconditionally, He abhors our sins. That is why a truly repentant sinner will be forgiven; but the unrepentant remains condemned. Sin is like a strong wind, made obvious only by its devastating effect on its surrounding. You don't see it, but you know it by its consequences.

The reality of sin today is found in its manifestations as poverty, hunger, sickness, disease, terrorism, and all manner of social, economic, and political injustices seen around the Globe.

You can always trace the origin of sin in the world back to Satan, a fallen angel, who rebelled but failed in his attempt to overthrow God. *Sin is not just a violation of God's law; it is an indication of evil in a society* (Isaiah 14; Ezekiel 2). In his delusion, Satan's goal was to destroy all of God's creation, including you and me. Although he could never overthrow God, he succeeded in luring mankind to rebel against their Creator; and that resulted in man's broken relationship with God. But God loves the world so much that He could not bear us separated from Him. And so He embarked on His restorative plan that sent Jesus Christ to the Cross, that whosoever believes in Him will not perish but be restored in an everlasting relationship with God the Father (John 3:16-17). Once a person accepts Jesus Christ as Lord and Savior, he becomes a member of God's family, the Ecclesia- the Church. This sacred opportunity to return to God is open to all regardless of gender, occupation, religion, social status, or race. But there can be no true repentance without a heartfelt confession of sin following admission of guilt:

1John 1:8-10 *If we say we have no sin, we deceive ourselves, and the truth is not in us. If we confess our sins, he is faithful and just, and will forgive our sins and cleanse us from all unrighteousness. If we say we have not sinned, we make him a liar, and his word is not in us.*

Proverbs 28:13 *He who conceals his transgressions [sins] will not prosper, but he who confesses and forsakes them will obtain mercy.*

:: ONLY JESUS CAN SAVE

Now only through Christ Jesus can you be restored back to God, for Jesus is the price God the Father paid for your redemption from the covenant of sin and death. Once restored, and filled with the Holy Spirit, you begin to see things through God's perspective. This translates into increased ability to draw a line of demarcation between good and evil. Thus it is through Christ that we receive the unique ability to truly understand the love of God as opposed to the love of the world; the peace that God gives as opposed to the peace that the world gives; the wisdom of God as opposed to the wisdom of this world; and relationship with God as opposed to religion.

In Christ, sin is not justified; it is forgiven. The sinner is acquitted [justified] not by his religious works or affiliation, educational status, wisdom, philosophy, political, economic or social status; but by Jesus paying the price for his sins. Thus God will not acquit anyone who refuses the free gift of Salvation, for the wages of sin is death (Romans 6:23). Unfortunately, this free gift of Salvation has been given a religious label called *Christianity*, which today is **no different from the religions of this world.**

:: SIN CREATES ACCESS TO CRISIS

Sin, individual or national, creates access to Satan, giving legal authority to oppression and torment. Sin is like a visa on a passport. It gives legal entry to an enemy who otherwise would have been illegal. The power of sin can be likened to a hammer by which the enemy gradually chips-away at your protective covering until it cracks open. Sexual sins, for instance, will make you prone to sexually transmitted diseases (STD). Just as personal sins weakens a person from inside out, creating an internal instability that renders a person prone to external attack, national sins will make a nation prone to destruction. It becomes even more dangerous when you allow Satan to work through your established government or judicial system to legalize abominable practices just as it is now happening in the United States and other nations.

Legalizing a sinful act will not make the act any less sinful. Sin is an act of rebellion against God, and will always be a snare to a people:

> **Proverbs 14:34** *Righteousness exalts a nation: but sin is a reproach to any people.*

Righteousness [*rightness, morality, honesty, justice, etc*] draws **Exaltation** [*praise, applaud, applause, favor, approval, etc*]. **Sin** [*crime, abominations, wrongdoing, transgression, etc*] draws **Reproach** [*blame, accusation, rebuke, scolding, criticism, affliction...*] to a nation.

> **Psalm 33:12** *Blessed is the nation whose God is the Lord...*

:: IGNORANCE, SINS, AND CURSES

Historically, the average age of the world's greatest civilizations is 200 years, with all of them coming to their ruins at the peak of their rebellion against God. The question remains as to whether America will beat the odds or not. The fact that sin will destroy a people is corroborated by other scriptures like Proverbs 29:4, 7, 14; as well as these words spoken through the Prophet Hosea:

Hosea 4:6-7 *My people are destroyed for lack of knowl-*

edge: because thou has rejected knowledge, I will also reject thee, that thou shall be no priest to me: seeing thou has forgotten the law of thy God, I will also forget thy children. As they were increased, so they sinned against me: therefore will I change their glory into shame.

Ignorance is the direct outcome of rejecting knowledge. To reject the knowledge of God is to reject God and reject the blessing of prosperity, liberty, and protection that He alone bestows. If a people reject God, God will reject them in return.

And if a people lack the knowledge of God, it will be hard for them to do God's will. Not doing God's will amounts to sinning against God. Now imagine a nation going from one generation to another **without making deliberate efforts** to pass on the knowledge of God. Soon, that nation will become Godless; and before you know it, here comes the wrath of God. Through the access created by sin, the enemy of righteousness penetrated the fabric of America, and sure enough, got a good number of people to reject the Knowledge of God.

Now many have become so desensitized to God. Science is good as long as it is not perverted. The concept of Evolution, so aggressively promoted, is one of the many attempts to further eliminate God from the society. Essentially, prayer has been kicked out of the School system; the Ten Commandments are fast being wiped out from public places. With abortion and same sex marriage basically legalized, the rest is history.

:: RIGHTEOUS LEADERSHIP AND GENERATIONAL BLESSINGS

Now if the people's overall will, judgment, decisions, and actions are pleasing to God, then the nation will be considered a righteous nation, blessed of the Lord; otherwise, it will be considered unrighteous, and cursed. Now more importantly, if the people in leadership or government act righteously, blessings will flow through them into the lives of the people; otherwise, curses abound:

> **Proverbs 29:2** *When the righteous are in authority [government] the people rejoice; but when the wicked rule [govern], the people groan.*

Righteous leadership is not about coming up with a bunch of superficial quick-fix social, economic, or political policies to mesmerize the people. Righteous leadership is about enforcing God's rulership to solve deep-rooted societal issues. Anybody can come up with programs, but only those who have the Spirit of God will lead their nation to destiny. Look around and see many nations, who, by corrupt legislations, have legitimized abominable practices and customs. Unfortunately most churches are yet to take a stand against unrighteousness. Today, many church leaders, afraid of criticism and rejection, continue to refrain from speaking out on pertinent societal issues. What then should we expect of a society whose churches are silent on important societal issues? Sadly, many Americans have bought into the unrighteous concept of *dualism* where their spiritual life is completely separate from their public life. This is where the stronghold of *Church and State Separation* takes its root. Dualism *suggests that your life in Christ should be completely separate from your public life. This is a doctrine of demons.* Please understand that God rules over everything; whether Church or State.

::CHAPTER NINE

SIN
AND
NATURAL DISASTERS

:: SPIRITUAL LAWS AND NATURAL LAWS

I believe there are at least two sets of laws governing the entire universe: natural laws and spiritual laws. These two distinct laws govern distinct but interfacing realms- *the natural and the spiritual realms*. Both realms have their origin in God, and are under God's Providence, for God is Spirit, and He is the origin of life. And so be it natural or spiritual, all have their origin in the Spirit:

> **Genesis 1:1** *In the beginning God created the heaven and the earth. And the earth was without form, and void; and darkness was upon the face of the deep. And the **Spirit of God** moved upon the face of the waters.*

With the spirit realm existing before the natural, I suggest to you that all natural laws have their *origin* in spiritual laws. Natural laws have their *domain* in the natural/physical realm, relating to the visible/observable part of the universe, having to do with the things we can see, feel, hear, smell and taste i.e. the five senses.

> **Hebrews 11:3** *Through faith we understand that the worlds were framed by **the word of God**, so that **things which are seen were not made of things which do appear.***

This is essentially why we are told that man shall not live (be sustained) by bread [natural sustenance] alone, but also by God's word [spiritual instructions (Luke 4:4)]. When we come to Christ, we begin to understand God's spiritual laws so as to live by them. The primary reason why Adam and Eve failed in the Garden of Eden was because they chose to ignore the instruction of God that *they must not eat of the tree of good and evil.* Their spiritual obligation was to leave that particular tree alone, but they chose to ignore that instruction.

Examples of natural laws are the laws of thermodynamics, gravity, osmosis, etc. Even though men may, from time to time, discover them, natural laws do not have their origins in man. All natural laws have their origin in the spiritual laws of God. Spiritual laws are superior to natural laws. Spiritual laws undergird and govern the physical world. Spiritual laws form the basis or foundation for the created world. Everything visible in this material world came out of the invisible eternal spiritual world. When both spiritual and natural laws are simultaneously in action, spiritual laws take precedence because they are superior to natural laws.

A person is said to be walking by Faith if he lives in this physical world but operates by God's eternal spiritual laws. A Miracle is said to occur when we employ God's spiritual laws to change our physical circumstances. This explains why Jesus could heal the sick, open blind eyes, feed 5000 people with 5 loaves and two fishes, and walk on water. By walking on water, Jesus used spiritual laws to defy the physical laws of gravity, density, and what not, to show that He is Lord over the entire universe. Jesus fully functioned as the Lord of both realms and taught us to do the same by faith.

What then is Faith?
Faith is the substantial, tangible means by which we are to live and function daily in a universe governed by both spiritual and natural laws. Jesus Himself, being the *author and perfecter* of our faith, is the only authority by which we can legitimately tap into the invisible reality of the spirit.

The name of Jesus brings a departure from the norm, with outcome transcending the laws of nature. Ironically, Hollywood calls it *6th* sense, depicting that it supersedes the five senses. Jesus Himself is a complete departure from the norm as He was supernaturally born in the flesh by a virgin, something that is naturally impossible. Jesus is not like Mohammed or Buddha who were born and buried like everyone else. Jesus is the supernatural Gift of God to supernaturally reconnect man with God the Father.

:: VIOLATING SPIRITUAL LAWS

God's laws are a gift to mankind, to guide us in living a fruitful righteous life on earth. Violation of these laws essentially tilts the *equilibrium of life* and brings about negative consequences that often take toll (short or long term negative impact) on our personal and national life. In His grand design, God, the creator of the universe, installed alarm systems designed primarily to limit, restrain, or overrule man's self-destructive activities. One of such is **God's Prophetic Voice**. History shows that people continually defy spiritual laws and ignore prophetic voices to their own detriment. The truth is, the God who is Love is also the God of Justice; He will never justify sin. In Christ alone is sin forgiven and iniquity removed. Sin not forgiven will be punished and iniquity not wiped away will be paid for. The question is, how will God punish national sins in this 21st Century?

According to the Prophet Nahum, some of the ways and means by which God revenges sin and cleanse the Land (environment) include tornado, deadly twisters, hurricane, cyclones, heavy rain, and floods; droughts and famine; earthquakes and volcanic eruptions; fire, furious fire, killer flames (including Thermonuclear), and powerful tremors to destroy acres of land, people, and properties. Whereas we call them natural disasters, the Bible describes them as God's response to the stench of sins in the world.

The first chapter of the Book of Nahum shows that God not only abhors sins, He also nurses grudge against sinful people, sinful businesses, sinful cities, and sinful nations. The character and nature of God demands that

He constantly eliminates sin from the land and deal severely with anyone/anything sold-out to sin. Thus the Lord would respond to a nation's accumulated sins by purging the land (Genesis 15). Depending on the severity of the sins, the Lord may purge a land by taking it away from its sinful occupants. He may also destroy it, partially or totally (Genesis 15, 18 & 19). Although this may, sometimes, bring temporary discomfort to righteous people, purgation is not meant to destroy good, but to destroy evil.

HEAVEN'S VENGEANCE ALTERS EARTH'S NATURAL BALANCE, TRIGGERING IRREGULAR GRAVITATIONAL PULL

Sin is not just a trait, it is a representation of the very person of Satan (Genesis 4:7). Every sin has a demonic personality or spirit behind it. For instance, murder is orchestrated by the demonic spirit of death, while jealousy is orchestrated by the demonic spirit of jealousy.

:: CORRELATION BETWEEN NATURAL DISASTERS AND PURGATION

There is a correlation between God purging sins from our environment and what we call natural disasters. Think about it, there is really nothing normal or natural about these disasters; they are triggered. Jesus Christ, the Lord of the Universe, says that the rapidly occurring disasters of this Century are part of the physical signs that this present corrupt world is about to end:

> **Luke 21:25** *And there shall be signs in the sun, and in the moon, and in the stars; and upon the earth distress of nations, with perplexity; the sea and the waves roaring...*

Violating God's laws releases the disruptive and destructive power of sin into the atmosphere. Sins, after much accumulation, trigger-off Heaven's vengeance. Heaven's vengeance released through the elements alters earth's natural balance, triggering irregular gravitational pull and unusual lunar phenomena. This, invariably, leads to unusual weather changes, irrational atmospheric temperatures, devastating wind patterns, and deadly earth movements that sometimes set-off great ocean surges, tsunamis. The point is, cycles of sin will continually trigger cycles of devastation. What we call natural disasters may very well be sin-induced disruptions of the natural balance of the ecosystems, often resulting in the destruction of the natural state of the environments in which we live. This brings us to the subject of Global Warming.

::CHAPTER TEN

GLOBAL WARMING AND HUMAN TRANSGRESSIONS

:: THE "GREENHOUSE" EFFECT

When Sunlight shines on the Earth's surface, it is first absorbed, and then radiated back into the atmosphere as heat. By His Providence, God has placed in the atmosphere gases, particles, water vapor, etc collectively called "greenhouse" gases that trap some of this heat while the rest escapes into outer space. This is the "greenhouse effect". "Greenhouse" gases allow in Sunlight, which, on striking the earth's surface, turns into heat. Some of the heat is retained to warm up the earth. Greenhouse gases include water (H_2O), nitrous oxide (N_2O), methane (CH_4), and carbon dioxide (CO_2). Together, these gases act like the glass in a greenhouse. By this devise, God has kept civilization developing within a consistent climate and has made life as we know it now possible.

:: GLOBAL WARMING CONCERNS

Incidentally, humans have increased the amount of "greenhouse" gases, especially carbon dioxide, by more than a third since the Industrial Revolution. The more greenhouse gases there are in the atmosphere, the more heat gets trapped. The more the heat, the more the earth's remaining ice sheets (Greenland and Antarctica) melts; and the more the sea level rises. Scientists are already seeing some of these changes happening faster than expected. In addition, scientists expect the following events to become even more frequent and widespread:

- Spreading of diseases,
- Bleaching of the Coral Reef,
- Heavy Rainfall,
- Heavy Snowfalls,
- Coastal Flooding,
- Prolonged Droughts, and
- Wild Fires.

This means more extreme weather, more intense major storms, more rain, longer and drier droughts (that severely challenge agriculture), and loss of fresh water from the glaciers. Think about it; these are the same elements by which God responds to sins in our societies.

:: REALITY OF GLOBAL WARMING

March 10, 2006:

Yahoo News reported that the *Bering Sea's* natural condition was being altered by global warming. The Bering Sea, the report says, covers more than 700,000 square miles, and is demarcated from the North Pacific Ocean by the Alaska Peninsula and Aleutian Islands. Considered to be one of the world's most productive fisheries, the northern parts of Bering Sea is a haven for sea ducks, gray whales, bearded seals, and walruses, all of which feed on cold-water critters.

Scientists have now discovered that the increasingly warm temperatures of recent years have caused this unique environment to change from Arctic to sub-Arctic conditions. This has led to the breaking and thinning of Ice.

The change in the ecosystems means change in the quality of sea ice due to warmer waters, turning the region to a haven for predator animals previously foreign to that part of the world. This report, among many others, drives home the point that Global Warming is truly a global reality.

March 2006: There were sightings of melting and collapsing Glacial Ice into the sea in Argentina. In that same month, Canada announced its warmest winter temperatures in recorded history since 1948. According to the Journal of Science, Global Warming will cause *animals to change in behaviors, Lakes to disappear, and Seas to rise.* Other direct manifestations of Global Warming include pronounced heat waves leading to unusually warm weathers and warmer global temperatures.

:: UNUSUAL RISE IN SEA LEVEL

February 27, 2006:
In an article titled, *"Has the Meltdown begun?"* TIME Magazine reports that scientists are worried that Greenland's Glaciers are melting faster than expected, and that the rates at which Glaciers are melting no longer fit into conventional global-warming scenarios. I suggest to you that this is because *our sins no longer fit into conventional*

scenarios. In other words, something unusual is happening in the world. Geoscientists are now suggesting that in places similar to the Eastern seaboard of the U.S., a 1ft. vertical rise in sea level means 100ft. recoil of coastline, and that if all the ice in Greenland melts into the Ocean, sea levels would rise by an **unbearable** 20ft.

In a separate report, NASA said that due to global warming, Antarctica has lost an unprecedented 152 cubic kilometers of Glacial Ice annually since 2002. The truth is many countries cannot withstand any unusual rise in sea level because the consequences are unimaginable. Scientists have suggested that as little as 1ft. vertical rise in sea level may cause many coastal cities around the world to be completely submerged. Bangladesh, they say, may disappear from the face of the earth. Many Islands would cease to exist; and who knows how much more inconceivable devastations may follow.

:: SOLAR STORM

In an approximately 11 year-cycle, the Sun reverses its magnetic field, producing a cycle marked by solar flares, sunspots and magnetic storms that have disruptive effects on Earth.

Monday, March 6, 2006:

According to the *New York Times*, scientists have now predicted that the next cycle of Solar Storm would be 30%-50% more intense than the last one. Solar storms are known to knockout power grids and damage communications systems. A more severe one would also endanger astronauts in space, disrupt air travel, and fill the earth with intense radiation.

Human activity, particularly the combustion of fossil fuels in cars, factories, and electricity production all result in Carbon Dioxide emission and other air pollution. This leads to a build-up of "greenhouse" gases that power the Global Warming trend. In the U.S., coal-burning power plants constitute the largest source of carbon dioxide pollution, producing 2.5 billion tons every year. This is followed by Automobiles that create nearly 1.5 billion tons yearly. Although we are told that technology exist now to modernize power plants, make cars that burn less gas, and generate electricity from non-polluting materials, I want to call our attention to the fact that our accumulated sins do more to bring about negative effects on our planet.

:: GOD COMMANDS SEASONS AND TIMES

Many scriptures explain the mysteries of Global Warming and its related phenomena. The Sun, Moon, and Stars being the primary heavenly bodies here are programmed under God's government to function in such a precise order to keep the planet Earth in functional and livable order:

Genesis 1:1 *In the beginning God created the heaven [the sky, the visible arch in which the clouds move, as well the higher atmosphere or heavens where the celestial bodies (spiritual beings) revolve] and the earth.*

Genesis 1:14-19 *And God said, Let there be lights in the firmament of the heaven to divide the day from the night; and let them be for signs, and for seasons, and for days, and years: And let them be for lights in the firmament of the heaven to give light upon the earth: and it was so. And God made two great lights; the greater light [the Sun] to rule the day, and the lesser light [the Moon] to rule the night: he made the stars also. And God set them in the firmament of the heaven to give light upon the earth, And to rule over the day and over the night, and to divide the light from the darkness: and God saw that it was good. And the evening and the morning were the fourth day.*

Psalm 104:19 *He appointed the moon for seasons...*

Jeremiah 31:35 *Thus saith the LORD, which giveth the sun for a light by day, and the ordinances of the moon and of the stars for a light by night, which divideth the sea when the waves thereof roar; The LORD of hosts is his name.*

What these scriptures are telling us is that God is the Creator of the heavens and the earth, and He is in charge of times and seasons. By His ordinances (decree, design, laws, order, rules…) the universe is sustained for our sake.

By His wisdom, God positioned the earth at a precise angle to the Sun and the Moon, as well as the Stars, to produce the suitable climatic conditions for humans, plants, and animals in the air, on the land, and in the seas. Seasons happen due to this tilt of the Earth's axis and the orbit of the Earth around the Sun. The earth's tilted axis of 23.5 degrees causes some parts of the earth to receive direct sunlight while other parts are receiving indirect sunlight via the moon. The seasons of the Northern and Southern Hemispheres are reversed, so that as the Northern Hemisphere is experiencing winter, the Southern Hemisphere is experiencing summer. Without the tilt, the Sun would always shine on the equator and no seasons would occur; plus a steady climate would exist across the planet; the region around the equator would always be hot; and the area around the poles would always remain cold.

If the angle of its axis was greater than 23.5 degrees, more of the earth's surface would be too hot, Polar Regions would melt, and oceans levels would rise. God set this planet in such a way that the interaction of the sun, moon, and earth would cause ocean levels to fluctuate. As the moon travels around the earth, and as both the moon and the earth travel around the sun, their gravitational force produces a lunar pull that causes the world's oceans to rise and fall. Hear what the Prophets have to say about this grand design:

Jeremiah 31:35 *Thus saith the LORD, which giveth the sun for a light by day, and the ordinances of the moon and of the stars for a light by night, which divideth the sea when the waves thereof roar; The LORD of hosts is his name:*

Psalm 89:9 *Thou rulest the raging of the sea: when the waves thereof arise, thou stillest them.*

Amos 8:9 *And it shall come to pass in that day, saith the Lord GOD, that I will cause the sun to go down at noon, and I will darken the earth in the clear day.*

Isaiah 51:15 *For I am the LORD your God, who stirs up the sea so that its waves roar- the LORD of hosts is his name.*

Jeremiah 5:22 *Fear ye not me? saith the LORD: will ye not tremble at my presence, which have placed the sand for the bound of the sea by a perpetual decree, that it cannot pass it: and though the waves thereof toss themselves, yet can they not prevail; though they roar, yet can they not pass over it?*

Scriptures admonish us to fear God; the One who sets limits for the seas and causes the waves to roar. Because these elements are all under God's control, it follows that they cannot get out of control or over-step their limits without God's approval.

:: STATE OF THE EARTH

Our spiritual condition determines **our physical conditions**. Therefore, our sins definitely affect the conditions of the planet, **the state of the earth**, and the condition in which **all created things exist.**

> **Genesis 6:7** *And the LORD said, I will destroy man whom I have created from the face of the earth; both man, and beast, and the creeping thing, and the fowls of the air; for it repenteth me (I regret) that I have made them.*

> **Genesis 6:13** *And God said unto Noah, The end of all flesh is come before me; for the earth is filled with violence through them; and, behold, I will destroy them with the earth.*

Sin alters the natural balance of the Ecosystem.

Sin will not only destroy a man, it will also corrupt his environment, making it less livable. That is why God would destroy a sinful man as well as his environment: for as the people are, so is their environment. That is why Revelation 22:1 tells us that the Lord will destroy this present corrupted earth, and bring forth a new earth and a new heaven, ushering in a new beginning:

> **Revelation 21:1** *And I saw a new heaven and a new earth: for the first heaven and the first earth were passed away; and there was no more sea.*

- *When God destroyed the people of Sodom and Gomorrah, He also turned their land into ashes, condemning them to extinction.*

- *In the time of Noah, God caused the flood to destroy the sinful, wicked, idolatrous, and adulterous people, wiping them out completely from the face of the earth.*

- *God will always save the righteous. The Ark of Noah prophetically points to Jesus, the Savior of the world. He always saves those who put their trust in Him.*

- *God did not spare the angels when they sinned, but committed them to pits of hell.*

- *He did not spare the ancient world, but preserved Noah (a preacher of righteousness) when He brought a flood upon the world of the ungodly.*

- *If by turning the cities of Sodom and Gomorrah to ashes, God condemned them to extinction, making them an example to the ungodly nations of today (2 Peter 2:4-11), what do you think He will do with 21st Century Sodomites?*

- *The people of Sodom & Gomorrah were exceedingly wicked homosexuals and idolaters (Genesis13:13). So the LORD rained upon them brimstone and fire [meteors] out of heaven (Genesis 19:24); and he overthrew all their farm lands, their natural resources, their citizens and immigrants, their produce and agricultural resources (Genesis 19:25-29).*

- *If the Lord did it six thousand years ago, what stops Him from doing it now? The whole world is now at a cross-road. Each and everyone will have to make a personal decision either to follow the Lord or take side with His enemies.*

:: GLOBAL WARMING: BIRTH-PAINS

There are increasing wars and rumors of war, terrors and terror threats; these signals are unmistakable; Global Warming is part of the birthing pains of the Last Days:

Luke 21:9-11 *But when ye shall hear of wars and commotions, be not terrified: for these things must first come to pass; but the end is not by and by. Then said he unto them, Nation shall rise against nation, and kingdom* *against kingdom: And great earthquakes shall be in diverse places, and famines, and pestilences; and **fearful sights** and great signs shall there be from heaven.*

Today, earthquakes, floods, and volcanic eruptions, apart from increasing in intensity, have also increased in occurrence. Scripture says that thunders and lightnings emanate from the throne of God (Revelation 4:5). Think about it, thunders and lightnings don't proceed to comfort anyone; they are elements of God's wrath. Right now it may be easy to imagine a farmland devastated by fire, but it is not easy to imagine a carnage resulting from a nuclear bomb explosion in your city; plus decades of unimaginable radiation. But we are living in the last days, and now anything is possible.

Are "Innocent" Children and Families Exempt from this Wrath? Unfortunately none is exempt. Nursing mothers, families, and children will be severely punished for the sins of their parents, government and politicians.

Luke 21:23-24 *But woe unto them that are with child, and to them that give suck, in those days! for there shall be **great distress** in the land [**nations**], and wrath [**God's anger**] upon this people. And they shall fall by the edge of the sword [**war**], and shall be led away captive [**refugees, prisoners of war, etc**] into all nations...*

Exodus 20:5 ... *for I the LORD thy God am a jealous God, visiting the iniquity of the fathers upon the children unto the third and fourth generation of them that hate me;*

One thing is for sure, God is in charge of the universe, and He has absolute command over the sun, moon, stars, the seas, the air, and the land. And whether He decides to use Meteors or Missiles, Storms or Tornadoes to respond to the misdeeds of men, He is also faithful to rescue His own children by the righteousness of Jesus Christ the Son of God:

Nahum 1:7 *The LORD is good, a strong hold in the day of trouble; and he knoweth them that trust in him.*

:: GLOBAL WARMING IN PROPHECY

I believe that the distress of many nations and the bewilderment now expressed by geoscientists was prophesied 2000 years ago by the Creator of the universe (Luke 21). I suggest to you that these disasters are sin-induced. It is our transgressions that made this world disaster-prone anyway; it was never like that in the beginning. However, because grace and truth came through Jesus, the gift of redemption is available to those who would take refuge in Jesus Christ; for the Bible says that those who put their trust in Him will be spared.

April 2007: The Clergy Debates:
In a vision by the Lord, I saw a debate in which the members of the clergy in America argued about the state of the nation with regards to the severe weather conditions (hurricanes, storms, fires, floods, etc); whether they are natural or induced. The members of the Clergy went back and forth and could not come to any reasonable conclusion. Then I saw the Hand of the Lord point to the first chapter of Nahum in my Bible, and prompted me to tell everyone that the prophecy in Nahum is being fulfilled even as we speak:

> **Nahum 1:2-8** *God is jealous [angry at sin], and the Lord revengeth [**punishes the sinner**]; the Lord revengeth, and is furious [**anger, hot displeasure, wrath**]; the Lord will take vengeance on his adversaries {**unrepentant people/nation**}, and He reserveth **wrath** for his enemies.*

I want all concerned clergy men and women to know that God nurses grudge against sin, and He promises to deal severely with sinful people, cities, and nations in many ways including the use of tornado, deadly twisters, hurricane, heavy rain, and floods (Nahum 1:3). The Lord will also use an overwhelming overrunning flood followed by utter darkness to overwhelm his enemies (Nahum 1:8). The Lord will also use Droughts and Famines, Earthquakes and Volcanic eruptions as signs of His displeasure towards sins (Nahum 1:4-5). Also,

the Lord will use Fire caused by Bombs and Thermonuclear Explosions to destroy acres of land and properties to show His indignation (Nahum 1:6). The Lord is
not limited in any way or shape or form. To show His
indignation, He may also use man-made instruments
including bombs and thermonuclear materials.

Typically, **when God uses volcanic eruptions and earthquakes** symbolically to speak to His Servants, it is to indicate an imminent upheaval, change, trial, judgment,
disaster, sudden violence, trouble, trauma, and shock; by
and large triggered by spiritual fractures in the societies
concerned. Like everything else, these activities all have
spiritual origins, references, and connotations. **And so
many of what we call natural disasters today are actually sudden disasters resulting from sin-induced disruptions in the ecosystems, upsetting the natural state of
the nations in question.**

:: ARISE BIBLICAL ENVIRONMENTALISTS

I suggest that we begin to pay close attention to the biblical connotations of what is going on in our environment; for there is nothing more natural for water than
for it to flow and stay its course within its banks. I want
you to know that it is not natural for water to overflow
its bank unless factors guiding its natural course are out
of balance (Jeremiah 5:22). Biblical Environmentalists
and Christ-centered Scientists must now arise and take

their rightful place to show forth the glory of God in the on-going debates about Global Warming and other related topics.

Now instead of confronting sin and its disruptive power as it continues to trigger devastations in all the nations of the world, we blame our disasters on the imaginary *Mother Nature*- who the heck is that? Mother Nature is the Idol with whom the kings of the earth have committed fornication, and the inhabitants of the earth have been made drunk with the wine of her fornication (Revelation 17:2). For all nations have drunk of the wine of the wrath of her fornication, and the kings of the earth have committed fornication with her, and the merchants of the earth are waxed rich through the abundance of her delicacies. And I heard another voice from heaven, saying, Come out of her, my people, that ye be not partakers of her sins, and that ye receive not of her plagues. For her sins have reached unto heaven, and God hath remembered her iniquities (Revelation 18:3-5).

To their own detriment, the nations of the earth have embraced this idol. Since they chose to give the glory of governing the Universe to an idol, God has now caused this same idol to be a snare to them (Judges 2:1-3). Yet, the LORD is good, a strong hold in the day of trouble; and he knoweth them that trust in him (Nahum 1:7).

::CHAPTER ELEVEN

RELIGION
VERSUS
SALVATION

:: AS IN THE DAYS OF NOAH

During the time of Noah, before the flood, man had not yet understood the devastating power of tsunamis, storm, heavy rain, and flood. Therefore, Noah, building an Ark as an act of obedience to God, looked foolish in the eyes of on-lookers. Now just as it was in the days of Noah when the people jeered the Ark, so it is today. Many people who mock the Gospel of Jesus Christ may be tempted to dismiss the dreams and visions I have so vividly described in this book. But as a watchman on the wall, my responsibility is to share this information with the American people and the nations of the world. And my message is that of the Love of God; not of *hate, division, or religious bigotry*. And this is my honest attempt to explain God's mind in human words. For the foolishness of God is wiser than the wisdom of all men put together (1Corinthians 1:19-25).

The Bible teaches that it was for freedom [liberty] that Christ has set us free (Galatians 5:1). Set us free from what? In Christ we have liberty, thus we are no longer subject to the yoke of religious bondage and manipulations. But the world's view of liberty is diametrically opposed to God's, hence God's wisdom, where the cross is concerned, has been gravely mistaken for foolishness-religion. For many ask, how could a man who died a humiliating death on a rugged cross (some two thousand years ago) save a soul today? But little do they know that the cross was actually the pivot of Jesus' mission (Isaiah 53:2-4), and was designed by God to be a stone upon which many will stumble. The cross would be a major offense to the established religions, philosophies, and intellectualism:

> **Romans 9:32-33** ...*For they stumbled at that stumblingstone; As it is written, Behold, I lay in Zion a stumblingstone and rock of offence...*

The wisdom of the cross was misunderstood even by the Jews as they itched for a Messiah that would save them primarily from the physical oppression they suffered in the hands of Roman imperialists. But Jesus' teachings pointed them to a new strategy- a strategy that really did not appeal to them:

> **Isaiah 8:14-15** *And he [Jesus] shall be for a sanctuary; but for a stone of stumbling and for a rock of offence to both the houses of Israel, for a gin and for a snare to the inhabitants of Jerusalem. And many among them shall stumble, and fall, and be broken, and be snared, and be taken.*

Even Jesus' first twelve disciples were for a while myopic and ignorant of the mission of the Messiah. As recorded in Acts 1:3-6, while He kept drawing their attention to the overall Kingdom, Purpose, and the Plan of God to save the world from self-destruction, they kept bothering

Him about their own little kingdom Israel. But as they continued to yield themselves to the revelatory will of God, they began to recognize His unmatched wisdom.

How it is that the world can predict the weather, gaze the stars, visit the planets, and fathom all kinds of mathematical mysteries, but fail to grasp the most important subject in life- the Gospel of Salvation.

The world nations have definitely stumbled as they continue to misrepresent and mischaracterize Jesus and His mission to the earth. Today, Jesus, as He did with the **Pharisees and Sadducees** of old, is now asking the scientists, politicians, philosophers, and religious elites of today: how it is that you can predict the weather, gaze the stars, visit the planets, and fathom all kinds of mathematical mysteries, but you cannot grasp *the Gospel of Salvation*, even as it relates to the desperate times in which we now live:

> **Matthew 16:1-3** ... *You know how to interpret the appearance of the sky, but you cannot interpret the signs of the times.*

I have to let you know that my intention in this book is not to knock any religion and label people as sinners; and it is not to suggest that status-quo Christianity is superior to any religion. What I am saying is that no religion or charity of any kind will save you from eternal damnation. For if religion could save and restore, there would have been no need to send Jesus to the rescue.

By the time Jesus came, the world definitely had more than enough religions. But the world desperately needed a Savior. That is why God sent Jesus to Save the World from the yoke of religious slavery (Galatians 5:1). Jesus came to save us from dead religions and worthless rituals. So we ought to rejoice in God's Victory.

:: JESUS CAN SAVE OSAMA BIN LADEN

Unfortunately, anyone seeking to know the *One True* God Almighty will have to first contend with religion, which, sadly, has entrenched its ugly self into the fabric of all societies. Although His name and mission have been grossly religionized, Jesus is not about religion. Everyone who seeks to come to Him must first of all come to terms with the fact that religion cannot save, and that they are coming to Jesus for a living relationship, not to a dead religion handed down by someone. And so to compare the Gospel of Jesus to any religion is really a disservice to God.

Religion is the work of man (the flesh), but Salvation is the work of God (the Spirit). Jesus is the Son of Promise, and all others are *products* of vain ambitions. And anything born of the flesh will always oppose (persecute) that which is born of the Spirit:

Galatians 4:28-30 *Now we, brethren, as Isaac was, are the children of promise. But as then he **that was born** after the flesh persecuted him that was born after the Spirit, even so **it is** now. Nevertheless what saith the scripture? Cast out the bondwoman and her son: for the son of the bondwoman shall not be heir with the son of the freewoman. So then, brethren, we are not children of the bondwoman, but of the free.*

Religion promises you salvation but only gives you bondage. You can never work to earn salvation; you can only receive it as a gift from God. Let me tell you how serious this is: the likes of Osama Bin Laden work religion all their life hoping to earn the love of God, but if they repent now and receive Jesus as Lord and savior, they will be saved. The souls of Muslims and all religious people and their so-called prophets are all thirsty/hungry for God. Unfortunately, because they are bound by religious spirits, they have all been eating and drinking from empty dishes. Religion has programmed them to believe that they can work, fight, and kill hard enough to earn a place in Heaven. They have been duped. Listen to what Jesus has to say:

> **Matthew 5:20** *For I say unto you, That except your righteousness shall exceed **the righteousness** of the scribes and Pharisees, ye shall in no case enter into the kingdom of heaven.*

The Sadducees, the scribes, the teachers of the law, and the Pharisees probably constitute the epitome of religious piety in the history of the world. They consider themselves to be the most pious of all people. Now Jesus is telling us that not even a religious piety as "great" as that of the Pharisees will save anyone. We are saved by the Grace of God through faith in Jesus Christ alone. Jesus also has a very serious message for those who call themselves Christians and are not Christians by heart (i.e. those who live by the flesh, with hearts far away from God):

> **Matthew 7:21** *Not every one that saith unto me, Lord, Lord, shall enter into the kingdom of heaven; but he that doeth the will of my Father which is in heaven.*

So you can see that this book is not about religious discrimination or racial hatred. It is not a case of Christianity versus Islam, Jews versus Gentiles, or Catholics versus Protestants. It is about my true and personal experience with God, of which I am now compelled to share, that you may not partake of the wrath that I see coming.

::CHAPTER TWELVE

RELIGION
AND
TERRORISM

For the sake of **political correctness**, government officials, and some others in business and entertainment refrain from publicly admitting that terrorism is pretty much connected to the religious ideology of Islam. Such people walk in denial and do not speak the truth because the truth is not in them. That is why many are fighting today's spiritual battles with physical weapons. The terror we all face today is a spiritual battle spurred even by religion. So it is impossible to truly fight the war on terror without addressing religion even as it relates to Islam.

RIDICULOUS: TERRORISTS BELIEVE THEY ARE KILLING INNOCENT PEOPLE AS A SERVICE TO GOD

Terrorism is synonymous with violence, bombing, and threats. What drives terrorists are the strongholds of evil spirits manifesting in religious ideologies that go far beyond ordinary imagination. The word of Jesus in John 16 gives us a profound insight to this oddity:

> **John 16:1-2** ...*indeed, the hour is coming when **whoever kills** you will think he is **offering service to God**.*

Terrorists believe that they are killing and shedding innocent blood as part of their service to God. This is ridiculous! Because they are ignorant and do not understand the love of God, it becomes very difficult for them to understand that they can never labor enough to earn God's love. There is no amount of blood a man can shed to earn God's love. Salvation is by God's grace, freely given by the death and resurrection of Jesus Christ.

Sadly, the Muslim world has been duped: they believe that they can earn their tickets to heaven/paradise by shedding innocent blood in honor of Allah. That is what their religion teaches. But Jesus said (in John 16:1-2) that Allah, to whom Muslims credit their "faith" (and to whom terrorists offer the blood of the innocent) is not God. So who then is Allah?

I assure you that terrorists are themselves victims of the religious spirit behind Islam. The Bible tells us in **2 Peter 2:19** that whatever controls you is what you serve and obey. Terrorists are under the influence and control of Satan, and they cannot but obey him. And as more Islam clerics openly or secretly spur their blood-mongering ideologies, religion will continue to be an instrument of division and terror in the world.

Hear terrorists in their own words:

January 30, 2006:
Al-Qaeda's No. 2 man Ayman al-Zawahiri appears in a video saying: *"Bush, do you know where I am? I am among the Muslim masses enjoying their care with Allah's blessings*

and sharing with them their "holy war" against you until we defeat you, Allah willing."

October 29, 2004:
Al-Qaeda's No. 1 terrorist Osama bin Laden begins his taped speech with *"Praise be to Allah...." And closes with "...Allah is our Guardian and Helper..."* In this particular speech, he used the word "Allah" 12 times, giving **Allah** all the credit for terrorism.

January 19, 2006:
Osama begins his taped speech with "Praise be to Allah..." In his speech, Osama uses the word "Allah" 12 times and credits Allah for the atrocities he committed.

In general, terrorists are known to shout, "Praise be to Allah", at the very climax of their suicide missions.

It is very obvious that these radicals attribute their wisdom and purpose to Allah. And there is no question that the God to whom Jesus lovingly restores mankind is not Allah to whom terrorists credit their atrocities. So who is Allah? Unfortunately, the world community has focused more on the ideology of the terrorists than on the spirit behind the ideology. That is why the whole issue of terrorism has been a myth to many people. To know why these terrorists do what they do, you have to know what spirit is at work behind the scene. I know that many people argue that Christians and Muslims worship the same God. But the scripture 1 John 4:1-3 commands us to not assume or believe that to be true; for many false prophets are now in the world to lure people to believe in demons. Once a society swallows *the bait of religion*, it becomes divided and ensnared; and the rest is history.

:: RELIGION: YEAST OF THE PHARISEES

Religion can be likened to *Yeast* that spreads quickly within a dough. Once a people bites into religion, the poison of religion spreads quickly among the people, and the society begins a gradual downward spiral towards social, economic, and political destruction. In no time, they will be forced into a compromise whereby they will have to take a little from the truth and a little from the lies. Today Satan is busy using all kinds of *distorted ideology of love, peace, and tolerance* to lure the American people to *compromise* their faith in God. Jesus particularly warned Christians to beware of **the yeast of the Pharisees:**

> **Matthew 16: 6** *Then Jesus said unto them, "Take heed and beware of the leaven (Yeast) of the Pharisees and of the Sadducees.*

> **Matthew 16: 12** *Then they understood that He did not tell them to **beware of the leaven of bread**, but **of the teaching** (false doctrines, abominations, pagan ideologies…) of the Pharisees and Sadducees.*

Religion actually started as a little yeast in the dough of Life in the *Garden of Eden.* For in the beginning, Adam and Eve had a pure undefiled relationship with God until the yeast came into their lives; no thanks to Satan. The same yeast that caused Adam and Eve to rebel against God then worked its way to the next generation causing Cain to kill Abel (Genesis 3 & 4). The same yeast continued its evil work among the Nimrodians, the Chaldeans, the Sodomites, the Egyptians, the Babylonians, the Arabians, the Grecians (Greeks), the Romans, and today's present world. The same yeast has also found its way into the Church, worldwide.

A little yeast in the dough will not remain unnoticed for long. In no time, evidence of fermentation will be seen. Sadly many people, just like their rebellious forefathers, continue in their futile attempt to unite the world through religions. They think that a bunch of religions in one pool will make everyone happy. This is what is called Pluralism. While I commend every effort to bring peace to the Middle East, I also understand that there can be no true peace either in the Middle East or anywhere else without the intervention of Jesus the Prince of Peace. **Religion is Yeast. It is an instrument of division. It can never unite; it can only divide.**

On the contrary, Jesus came to save us from dead religions and worthless rituals; to unite us in Him, and restore us to a true relationship with God, our Father.

Fermentation:

According to Webster's Dictionary, **a leaven or yeast** is any influence or addition that causes a general change or modification to the whole. It does not matter how much dough you have, a little yeast (of religion) will cause even a great nation like America to change in structure and composition- a process called **fermentation**.

Biologically speaking, yeast consists of minute fungus cells. These cells, under the right temperature and pressure, grow extremely rapidly within the dough. As they multiply, they alter the structure and composition of the dough. As they penetrate the entire fabric of the dough, they break the bonds between the molecules of the dough, causing the whole dough to break up and disperse. This is exactly how the yeast of religion works; and truly it has effectively worked its way into the heart of America and all the nations of the world.

Religion has caused many Christian nations to become spiritually bankrupt, opening them up to demonic assault (even external aggression). Not even the Church is immune to the attack of the yeast of religion.

Because the Yeast of Religion penetrated the Church, **the finished work of Jesus Christ** has thus been misconstrued as one of the many religions of the world. And so instead of many nations winning the heathens over to the Kingdom of God, the heathens have won them over to the kingdom of darkness. The Lord warned against the deception of religion, saying:

> **Deuteronomy 11:16-17** *Take heed lest your heart be **deceived, and you turn aside and serve other gods and worship them**, and the anger of the LORD be kindled against you, and he shut up the heavens, so that there be no rain, and the land yield no fruit, and you perish quickly off the good land which the LORD gives you.*

:: FERMENTATION AND TERRORISM

When the Yeast of Religion ferments, Terrorism breaks out! Now the word "fermentation" or "ferment" is synonymous with confusion, agitation, commotion, disorder, chaos, havoc, and uproar. Think about it, these same horrible words convey the very spirit of terrorists and terrorism. So, wherever you see terrorism break out, there you will find the underlying spirits of confusion, agitation, commotion, disorder, chaos, havoc, and uproar.

As you will read in subsequent chapters of this book, these spirits require human vessels to perpetuate their evil deeds. This is where religious people come in. Religious people make themselves readily available for these spirits to use them to carry out their evil deeds. Therefore, do not be religious, but aspire to have a personal relationship with God through His Son, Jesus Christ.

::CHAPTER THIRTEEN

ISLAM
AND
TERRORISM

:: PERSONAL EXPERIENCE WITH ISLAM

I grew up seeing many people look up to my mom for encouragement and godly counsel. A humble and kind-hearted woman, mom was born of the tribe of *Itsekiri in Mid-West Nigeria*. Kind to a fault, she raised and cared for more children than she ever had of her own. Gener-

MY MOM'S LIFE WAS GROSSLY SUPPRESSED AND SUBORDINATED ON ACCOUNT OF ISLAM.

ous; mom would give and give until there was nothing left. Unfortunately mom had no choice than to live her 39 years of married life under the siege and bondage of Islam. As a youngster, I witnessed, first hand, the abuses my mom suffered in the name of Islam. She was controlled and manipulated, and enslaved physically and mentally by the generality of my dad's extended family who justified their actions by Islamic religious beliefs. My mom did not enjoy her married life; her joy was stifled and her business aspirations crippled. She was grossly suppressed and subordinated on account of *Islam*, which incidentally, means *submission, surrender, or give in.*

To worsen the matter for her, she had a permanent status as my dad's youngest wife- *a position that rendered her no better than a dignified slave*. The point is, mom married into a religious ideology/culture that has little or no respect for women's dignity. My mom is only one in the hundreds of millions of victims of Islam in Nigeria, West Africa, the Middle East, and other regions of the world. As the last son of my dad's, I ranked twelfth among fifteen children. I witnessed, first hand, mom's sleepless nights and deprivations, anguish and despair; but there was not much I could do to help her. Many a time I wanted to rebel against my dad's house for mistreating my mom, but mom would stop me right in my track. I often suggested she divorce my dad, but she always said to me, "I will stay the course for your sake."

Consistent with Islam, my dad (now late) practiced polygamy, with an extended family structure of four wives and one or two concubines at any given time. Now it will interest you to know that just like many religious people try to cover-up their dark, empty, and unfulfilled lives with good-works of charity, my dad religiously devoted his life to public service, serving many years as a police superintendent and later as a Magistrate Judge.

He was well known for arbitrating in all kinds of communal disputes, and regularly gave alms to help those in need. Unfortunately, good works can never substitute for righteousness (the right to stand justified before God). Religion wants you to believe that you have to *work* your way to heaven. *Moderates* like my late dad believe that *good-works* such as helping the poor and getting involved in community development is a ticket to heaven.

Extremists and radicals like Osama bin Laden and his world-wide terror crew believe that shedding the blood of innocent Christians and Jews is a sure way to earn a seat next to God. These are some of the lies religion has caused many to believe. I want you to know that Good-works will neither earn you peace with God nor a place in heaven. By the time my dad died in 1986, he left me with much religion, but no relationship with God.

:: RELIGION VERSUS RELATIONSHIP

In 1985, I graduated with a Bachelors degree in Bio-chemistry from the University of Ibadan, Nigeria. Although I had a relatively good job, I was lonely, and my life was miserable, empty. I had no real hope for the future, let alone the hereafter. Of course I didn't know why until Jesus rescued me. Just like my dad, my destiny was buried under the religious spell of Islam. It took Jesus to blow wide open my religious cover; for dad passed away at a time when I needed a father the most. My whole life literally fell apart at his departure. Life became even more complicated as mom was moved to a separate location to mourn one year. I had never been that lonely in my life. Essentially, I became *orphaned.*

To be orphaned is to be without parents: to lack the love of God the Father- to lack the good care, guidance, purpose, and sense of belonging that comes from Him alone.

This was definitely the most critical stage of my life- the defining moment that broke my religious cover, and opened my eyes to the reality of my spiritual condition. Looking back now, I am convinced that the inner strength, revelation, and sense of purpose that saw me through that crucial stage of my life came not from religion, but from the Lord Jesus Christ.

I have no doubt that collapse is imminent and inevitable for any person, community or nation that trusts in religion or any other thing except the Lord. Man is incomplete without a personal relationship with God. Jesus is our link to God. Life without Jesus creates **Spiritual Deficiency**- a deficit we all try to fill with material things and idols. Without proper biblical knowledge and understanding, one most definitely will fall into material and spiritual idolatry.

Religion will cause you to look up to created things, instead of the Creator of all things. God is our source of life and provision; and our sense of worth and validation must come from Him. Just like many people today, I once looked to career, people, and false gods for answers to life's intriguing questions. For that reason, my life lost meaning, direction, and sense of destiny. I began to wander in a maze of emptiness and purposelessness; the same reason why many people, rich and poor alike, die without finding/fulfilling their purpose. Please understand that the God I am talking to you about is neither the god(s) our spiritually bankrupt ancestors left behind nor is He the imaginary ones we have created for ourselves. He is the God of Abraham, Isaac, and Jacob; Creator of Heaven and earth.

:: IN DESPERATE SEARCH FOR GOD

Three years following my dad's death, my life was characterized by a desperate search for God. In my desperation, I visited a number of religious settings including some "dead" churches, mosques, and shrines. I soon found out that these religious leaders were no more than blind guides and dignified soothsayers. But out of ignorance, I continued to walk that destructive path until I had an encounter with Jesus Christ.

I assure you that your herbalists and spiritualists [**psychics, mystics, telepathists, diviners, fortune tellers, mediums, and mind-readers**] are nothing but blind guides who know next to nothing about God. All they want is your money and your life to control. They will cause your life to be overwhelmed by pressure, driven by fear, and consumed by *the need* to know your future and manipulate your destiny- a subject called **Divination and Occultism.**

Divination **capitalizes on humans' uncontrolled desire to know the future, while the** *Occult* **capitalizes on humans' desperation to manipulate the future.**

:: DIVINATION AND OCCULTISM IN
MAINSTREAM SOCIETY

Divination and Occult are two deadly weapons by which Satan continues to hold the world captive. The book of Deuteronomy 18:9-13 classify as abominations such practices *as child molestation/child killing/abortion (Leviticus 20: 25); divination, sorcery [contacting the spirit world either to foretell the future], interpreting omens, casting spells, psychic activities, and consulting the dead.*

God wants to progressively reveal the *future* to you but only through His righteous means, most of which I have earlier discussed. Sadly, as we often demonstrate an unrestrained desire to know and control the future, many people have become exceptionally fascinated by *horoscopes, fortune telling, witchcraft, the galaxies,* even science and technology. It is the same reason why Eastern Mysticism, New Age cults, white magic, black magic, white witches, black witches and many other abominations have all mesmerized America and bewitched the whole world. Many like Harry Potter who make billions of dollars in profit from witchcraft and occult movies, books, clothing, and accessories may not agree with me, but soon the world will come to understand that all these evil practices arise from evil imaginations orchestrated by Satan the master of all deceptions (Deuteronomy 4).

:: "ANGELS" OF LIGHT

Therefore, it is not strange to see Satan and his demons disguise as servants of righteousness (2 Corinthians 11:15), with countless of them operating in various capacities in diverse places in the world. Their goal is to perpetuate and propagate all kinds of negative and ungodly influences in our social, economic, political, and spiritual life. Satan is the illegal duplicator who uses his perverted knowledge of the spirit realm to manipulate our imagination and thoughts in order to destroy our identity and destiny; for as a man thinks in his heart, so he is (Proverbs 23:7a).

The Bible in 2Corinthians 11:14 describes Satan as a dark angel who disguises himself as a messenger of light to mislead people. Satan understands that humans have an innate desire to know the truth and have the knowledge of God. He also knows that people in their right minds will not seek false prophets and liars for counsel. So what does he do? He sets up a façade of religions, having the appearance of godliness but lacking God's character and nature.

God does not want us to be manipulated (Proverbs 16:4, Psalm 149:4). He wants us to have the right imagination about Him, about ourselves, and about the world in which we live. He takes personal responsibility and pleasure in imparting us with the true revelations about

Himself and ourselves so we can have the right perspectives about life. Jesus came to restore us to God's purpose and will; so it only makes sense to put our life in His care. In Exodus 7:10-12, we see how Pharaoh's magicians also turned their rods into snakes just like Moses (the servant of God) did. God's supremacy was demonstrated as Moses' snake swallowed up the snakes of the magicians. In the book of Acts, we also see an interesting drama unfold:

> **Acts 16: 16-18** *And it came to pass, as we went to prayer, a certain damsel possessed with a **spirit of divination** [snake] met us, which brought her masters much gain [money] by **soothsaying**...*

The long and short of this story in Acts 16:16-18 is that Satan's spirit was cast out of the girl by Apostle Paul only **in the name of Jesus; not in the name of Mohammed, Buddha, Confucius, Shinto, or anyone else.** The girl was completely set free from the devil and the devil's money-making machine destroyed. But look around you today, divination and occult continue to generate hundreds of billions of dollars in revenue from books, movies, games, etc not only because the world continues to ignore the knowledge of God, but more so because Christians are failing in their sacred duty to demonstrate God's Power to the world. For this lack of knowledge, many are destroyed (Hosea 4:6), and many end up in hell. By the way, hell is real, even if you don't believe it. At age 22,

God showed me what my ultimate destination would be if I die as a Muslim. I caught a glimpse of hell; trust me, you don't want to go there.

:: A GLIMPSE OF HELL

1987: My Escape from the Pit

It was a huge procession, probably billions of people, all moving rapidly down a valley towards a pit. We were headed down into that formidable place called hell. I did not see the inside of the pit but I could feel its destructive power as we got closer to it. There was an invisible force that kept us moving down toward that valley; and none of us could change course, run, or escape. I noticed that the sky was very angry and the clouds were roaring mad. We had no control, whatsoever, of where we were headed. My hands were bound together; so were my legs. I was handcuffed and shackled by invisible handcuffs and chains. As condemned sinners, we headed helplessly down to hell; our fate was sealed. I was so terrified. I looked up and noticed that even the sky was angry at us. I asked why the sky was roaring mad at us, and a voice from heaven answered, saying, "it is the wrath of God". At that I became even more terrified. Then all of a sudden I saw a big Hand (which I know is the hand of God) pull me out of the hell-bound procession, sit me on a chair, and put a wooden cross in my hand. And in a very stern tone, I heard the voice of God say to me, "Now Preach!" Then I woke up.

Initially, I didn't understand the gravity of this revelation even though I realized that it was the cross that rescued me from the hell to which I was headed. But now I know better.

:: SPIRITUAL DEFICIENCY OF THE ARABS

Attributable to spiritual deficiency, my orphan experience as a Muslim is a microcosm of the intense **orphan spirit** militating against the Muslim world wherein the Islam spirit has afflicted people of Arab descent with inherent despair, anger, and frustration. For one, Muslims are the **descendants of Ishmael**. Ishmael was Abraham's eldest son by **Haggai- Abraham's** concubine (Genesis 16:3; Genesis 21:5). According to God's covenant promise to Abraham, Isaac (the free-born child of promise) was the covenant child; and Ishmael (the slave-born) was not (Galatians 4:24). Although God intended to bless Ishmael and make him also into a nation (the Arabs), He required of Ishmael to submit to His covenant plan for Isaac. But instead of Ishmael to humble himself and yield to the perfect will of God, he rebelled not only against God *the Father* but also against Abraham, his natural father. By so doing, he alienated himself from the inheritance. Thus he and his Arab descendants became orphaned; alienated from God's perfect will.

Though Muslims are very religious, they lack the true nurturing that comes from God the Father.

Easton Bible Dictionary explains that Ishmael grew up a true child of the desert, wild and wayward; like a wild ass among men (Genesis 16:12). Ishmael's rude and wayward spirit broke out in expression of insult and mockery against Abraham (Genesis 21:9-10). His vicious anger and jealousy towards Isaac eventually got him and his mother Haggai thrown out of the patriarchal life (Genesis 21:14-16). Viciously angry, Ishmael departed and settled in the land of Paran, a region lying between Canaan and the mountains of Sinai where he became a great archer (Genesis 21:9-21).

The Dictionary further describes Ishmael as becoming **a great desert chief having a troop of wild retainers and half-savage allies.** He had twelve sons, who became the founders of so many **Arab tribes or colonies.** These are the Ishmaelite that spread over the wide desert spaces of Northern Arabia from the Red Sea to the Euphrates (Genesis 37:25; 37:27-29; 39:1). With his hand against every man, and every man's hand against him, Ishmael plotted against Gedaliah, and treacherously put him and others to death, carrying off many captives. Thus terrorist Ishmael portrayed characteristics similar to those of the *terrorists* of today.

Whatever is born of the flesh will rise up against that which is born of the Spirit (Galatians 3:27-29). Ishmael was born of the flesh; Isaac was born of the Spirit. While Isaac is a prophetic type of Jesus, Mohammed, Buddha, and the rest of them are all type of Ishmael for they were all born of the flesh. It is no surprise therefore that they all rose up to persecute Jesus- the true Son of God. And as their leaders have persecuted Jesus, so will their followers persecute Jesus' true followers.

:: SPIRITUAL PROFILE OF TERRORISTS (DISINHERITED & ALIENATED)

Disinherited, alienated, and angry, one can only imagine the ruthlessness of Ishmael. Through the ages, this ruthlessness has been transmitted to his Arab descendants.

According to the *American Heritage Dictionary of English Language: Fourth Edition 2000*, **an orphan feels an affinity with other parentless children.**

This explains the unmatched solidarity and quest for recognition shared by Muslims all over the world. Did you notice the protests over the Mohammed's cartoon? The riots broke out February 2006 in Syria and spread out like wild-fire to the Muslim nations. This is a typical and vivid portrayal of the *orphan spirit-motivated* kinship demonstrated by Muslims all over the world. But God has remained faithful to everyone, even the Muslims. He has not forsaken any of us. Instead, He made a way of escape for us through the death and resurrection of Jesus Christ. Abraham, Isaac, and Jacob (Israel) are the human ancestors of Jesus Christ.

Through Jesus and His followers, God has also extended His Grace to the Gentiles (Arabs inclusive). The Abraham covenant blessing of the Jews is now available to the rest of the world so that no one is left out of God's family (Genesis 12 & 17, Galatians 3:13-14). So you see that Jesus died for everyone, including the Muslims. Anyone who is not in Christ is automatically alienated from this promise of life here now and hereafter. Just like it was offered to me, the same covenant of life is also offered to all Muslims today.

You may have noticed that in spite of their vast wealth, many Arabs/Muslims still feel politically disadvantaged, socially marginalized, and spiritually alienated from the rest of the world. This is because their souls long for a love-based relationship with God; that which no religion can give them. As spiritual orphans, angry, and searching for love, acceptance, and self-worth, many Arabs/Muslims continue to perceive life through a kaleidoscope of ungodly religious ideologies.

And because many of them feel socially marginalized and politically disadvantaged, they are predisposed to "terrorist causes" that look to validate their quest for justice and equity without regard for divine plan and purpose.

Terrorists are driven by deep-rooted worthlessness and anguish of the soul. And as they continue in their futile quest for "justice and equity", their resentment towards their Christian brothers continues to escalate. And there comes a time when their internalized anger becomes externally expressed in violence and murder. Ultimately, their desire is to destroy the Jews and wipe out all Christians. Thus many have become terrorists, and even many more have the potential to become terrorists.

::CHAPTER FOURTEEN

SPIRIT OF ISLAM 1
(THE GREAT DECEPTION)

Millions of Muslims have questions about their religion, but they are not able to express their concerns publicly because they have been suppressed by religious pressure. You must understand that in Islam, there is nothing like choice or freewill. Majority of Muslims are so-called not because they chose to be, but because they are forced to be. And many are Muslims simply because they were born or raised by parents entrenched in Islamic culture and tradition. I was once like them- a victim of religious circumstances. Even as a young man, I couldn't comprehend Allah; he was distant and abstract. You couldn't have a personal relationship with Allah; it is simply impossible. You simply have to follow the rituals, day in day out; no questions asked. You had to simply accept what the clerics say; and you can't question them either. And so I came to the conclusion that Allah is fundamentally different from the *One* true God of the Bible.

It will interest you to know that it is forbidden to translate the Koran from Arabic to other languages. Think about it: what book can be so sacred that you couldn't translate it so people can read and relate? The truth is, if you read and understand the Koran, you will question its content; and *the clerics* don't want that to happen. So their goal is **not for you to understand the words of the Koran, but for** you **to simply memorize them and do exactly what they (the Clerics) say.** When I was young, dad enrolled us at an *Islamic After-School Program (Ile-Kewu* in Yoruba language). All we did there was memorize words that we did not even understand. Thank God we were thrown out of the program within a few weeks because my brother *Ladi* always got into a fight with other students in the program.

Today, many Muslims who read to understand the words of the Koran fail to challenge its contents because they are compelled to take pride in it and defend it, even if it means shedding their blood. The point is, if you challenge the Koran, the clerics will call you a blasphemer, and behead you. It is death to you if you renounce Islam and become a Christian. Under the Sharia law, renouncing Islam is a capital offense which carries the death penalty.

A case in point is the trial of Abdul Rahman (a 41-year-old former Medical aid worker) who faced the death penalty for becoming a Christian under Afghanistan's Islamic laws. The trial invited much international outcry: U.S. President George W. Bush said he was "deeply troubled" by the case; and U.S. Secretary of State Condoleezza Rice telephoned President Hamid Karzai on March 23, 2006 to seek a "favorable resolution" of the case. Muslim clerics wanted Abdul Rahman hanged or beheaded; and they promised an uprising (similar to the one against Soviet occupying forces in the 1980s) against American occupation if their government failed to kill Abdul Rahman. Now if in 2006 majority of Afghans would advocate killing a man simply because he chose to become a Christian, then you know that the nation of Afghanistan is not yet free. For true freedom begins in the soul. A soul free from religion will be free indeed.

I find it very interesting that many who call themselves Muslims don't even read the Koran let alone understand its content. I know this to be true because I still have hundreds of relatives who call themselves Muslims; they are simply cosmetic. What they all have is superficial piety fashioned after their leader Mohammed. I love them dearly, and I pray daily for their salvation.

:: MOHAMMED, MECCA, AND THE KORAN

Whereas the God of the Bible says you shall have no God except Him, and you shall not worship the sun, moon, stars or bow down to any image (Deuteronomy 4:19), billions of Muslims worship the moon, paying yearly homage to the Ka'abba in Mecca to worship, kiss, and bow down to a black stone. Five times daily, they bow down to a false god, chanting words they have no understanding of. Historically, this black stone, representative of Allah is one of the over 250 tribal gods worshipped among the Arabs even during the time of Mohammed. The story that Mohammed received his revelations from Angel Gabriel while meditating in a cave is not true. This falsehood is revealed even in the type of meditation Mohammed was engaged in. Soon you will understand what I mean.

Biblical Meditation versus Satanic Meditation:
The primary characteristic of Biblical Meditation is that the person is actively engaged i.e. **physically & mentally conscious** as he or she studies, prays, and considers the Word of the Lord in the Bible. This is godly meditation.

Biblical meditation is different from the other type of meditation in which a person is **charmed**, and subjected to **an altered state of consciousness** in order to experience a "union with god or a spirit being". The truth about this demonic practice is that many people who claim to be getting in touch with **god, angels, or higher powers** are actually communing with demons in the spirit realm. An example is the Mantra mind-altering transcendental meditation in which **a demonic phrase or chant is repeated over and over again to blind the person's mind, hypnotizing him, and opening him up to the spirit world.** Listen to what Jesus says about it:

> **Matthew 6:7** *But when ye pray, use not vain repetitions [repeated words or phrases], as the heathen [pagans/idolaters] do: for they think that they shall be heard for their much speaking [repeated chants].*

Muslims and Catholics use many forms of rosary for repeated chants. According to the Holy Bible, this is a heathen practice. New Age spiritualists have now modernized ungodly meditation, re-packaging it into the so-called **New-Age Therapy.** They now use modern forms of *slow songs, liturgical melodies, whispered ritualistic prayers, demonic sounds, yoga tricks, drugs, psychic spells* and other kinds of mind-altering techniques of Hinduism and Eastern Mysticism as a means of achieving an altered state of consciousness. This is **a mystical state that releases the control of one's mind to Satan.**

:: THE SCIENCE OF UNGODLY MEDITATION

On May 7, 2001, *Newsweek* Magazine published an article titled, *"Religion and the Brain".* This article reported on a number of scientific researches conducted to find out what happens during a spiritual or mystical experience induced by an **uplifting ritual, a sacred music, slow chanting, elegiac liturgical melodies and whispered ritualistic prayer.** According to the experiments, the typical responses of the individual *meditators* include a feeling of:

• Without boundaries and connection with energy
• Openness, nothingness; oneness with everything
• Existence outside time and space
• A profound letting go of the boundaries
• A profound sense of connection to everything
• Not being able to distinguish or separate things
• Communion, peace, openness to experience...
• Emergence of true inner self
• Timelessness and Infiniteness
• Being part of everyone and everything in existence;

- Fullness of the presence of a "deity"
- Hearing the singing of the planets…
- Being the "light", relaxing the mind
- Going out to infinite space and returning
- An intense feeling of "love"

The truth is, in a mystical state, your orientation and judgments are altered, making you vulnerable to the spirit world. Your choices, course of action, points of reference, views, line of reasoning, understanding, and clear-mindedness become misrepresented, distorted, and foggy because you lose control of your spirit. The claim of Scientists, according to this report, is that in a mystical experience, there is a fading of the content of the mind and a decline in sensory awareness. Interestingly, the claims of the *meditators* and the reports of the scientists are very much in line with the claims of the Scriptures **1 Timothy 4:1** and **Proverbs 25:28**:

> **1 Timothy 4:1** *Now the Spirit speaks expressly, that in the latter times some shall depart from the faith, giving heed to seducing spirits, and doctrines of devils;…*

According to *Strong* Dictionary, the word "Seducing" refers to a Greek word "planos" (plan'-os) meaning **roving (as a tramp)**, i.e. (by implication) an impostor or a misleader; deceiver; seducer. Seducing spirits are demons; counterfeit spirits that try to mimic God. Kicked out of heaven because of their rebellion, they now **rove about**

as tramps, seducing ignorant humans via their perverted knowledge of the spirit realm.

The word "Doctrine" refers to the Greek word "didaskalia" (did-askal-ee'-ah) meaning instruction, learning, teaching. Satan's goal is to establish his own teachings, doctrines, and instruction manual- **a false bible** with which to indoctrinate ignorant humans, mislead them, and enrol them in hell.

:: YOUR MIND: THE GATE TO YOUR SOUL

Devils/demons are spirit beings capable of impersonating *the Divine* to the itching ears of the ignorant who is seeking truth in the wrong places. Once demons gain access into your mind, they start to influence your thoughts and actions. Depending on their mission, they begin to influence your reasoning, speech, and composition; working in you and through you to live out their perverse life of murder, rage, anger, theft, orgies, murder, pedophilia, homosexuality, etc. Listen, the devil will even write through you if you let him.

Look around, and you'd find numerous books, movies, ornaments, apparels, and video games all motivated by Satan. There are also many social, political, economic, educational, social, and religious systems orchestrated by the devil in many societies. It will interest you to know that every sin, sickness, disease, wickedness, etc

all have their corresponding demonic ties in satanic personalities. Due to his anti-Christ nature, the devil's goal is to defile, distract, deceive, oppress, suppress, possess you and bring you under his rule. I suggest that you don't let him. You are too precious and too important to God to allow yourself to fall into that kind of cheap religious deception.

::CHAPTER FIFTEEN

SPIRIT OF ISLAM 2
(DEMONIC INFILTRATION)

We have established the fact that in a state of **altered consciousness**, a person's moral judgment, thoughts, conscience, and orientation are altered or completely negated. In this state, the person has apparently lost control of his life to demons. Thus he becomes like a remote controlled robot or a hanging quill that readily gives-in to any slight influence or push from wind or man. If you have ever been drunk on alcohol or have ever been under the influence of a drug or any form of sedation, then it probably will be easier for you to understand what I am trying to say here.

Consider this scripture:

> **Proverbs 25:28** *He that hath no rule [authority or control] over his own spirit [mind] is like a city that is broken down, and without walls.*

Your mind is the very gate to your soul. Once you lose control of your mind, your judgments become altered, and your very life becomes open to the influence of evil spirits. These evil spirits will control you at random and cause you to act in whichever way they so please according to the will of Satan their master. That is why a person under the influence of evil spirits cannot freely live for God. Please understand that Demons don't voluntarily depart from a person, place, or thing; they have to be cast out, and that is possible only in the name of Jesus (Matthew 8:31). Demons can never be cast out in the name of Mohammed, Buddha, or other religious names because these are mere men. Jesus is the one that is above all names, powers, and principalities.

Unfortunately many preachers are themselves under the influence of demons. Thus their spiritual judgments are distorted and their personalities altered. And so the exercise of their legitimate spiritual right is also diminished.

:: THE SPIRIT BEHIND THE KORAN
(Ref Encyclopedia of Religious Knowledge)

Recall that evil spirits answer to Satan, and cause a person under their influence to act out Satan's will. With that in mind, let me now share with you what probably is the most profound revelation the Muslim world needs to have. I was at the prayer garden in 2004 when the Lord led me to research this information, which can be referenced in the *New 20th-Century Encyclopedia of Religious Knowledge (2nd Edition):*

On pages 483-484, concerning the Messages of the Koran, the Encyclopedia clarifies that the messages of the Koran, believed by Muslims to be holy word of Allah, was given to Mohammed with Mohammed having no choice in deciding the time, location, content, or vocabulary of the information he received.

On page 606, concerning Automatic Writing, it explains that this is the dictation or writing done in a trance state; without the physical and mental consciousness of the writer.

I believe that these pages of the *Encyclopedia* offer a profound insight as to exactly how Mohammed received the words of the Koran. True followers of Christ know that we humans are no robots who automatically do whatever God says. We are uniquely created by God to be intelligent, conscious, thinking beings that can reason, make individual choices, consider our decisions, and judge our actions relative to God's Laws and commands. This unique quality was not demonstrated in the relationship between Mohammed and the creature that gave him the words of the Koran.

Mohammed, an illiterate, who could not read or write went into a cave to meditate on what scripture? Certainly not the Holy Bible! As he continued to engaged in ungodly meditation, in a state of altered consciousness, a Jinni- a demon who claimed to be angel Gabriel possessed him, and by automatic dictation, the demon gave him the blasphemous anti-Christ words of the Koran. Except by automatic dictation/writing, Mohammed, an illiterate, could not have had the capacity to become the memory bank of Allah to transmit hundreds of pages of document to other scribes.

It will interest you to know that such occult practices as automatic writing, automatic dictation, astrology, numerology, palm reading, fortune telling, and contact with dead, discarnate (disembodied) personalities, mediums and trance channeling were common evil practices among the Arabs even during the time of Mohammed when the Arabs predominantly worshipped over 250 false gods, the most prominent of which was Allah.

Now if you have seen the 1990 movie *Ghost*, then what I am saying will be easier for you to understand. The character *Oda May Brown* [played by Whoopi Goldberg] was the medium through which the ghost of *Sam* Wheat [played by Patrick Swayze] acted out his desire for his wife *Molly Jensen* [played by Demi Moore]. Of course there are hundreds of other movies that also portray this oddity. I submit to you that Islam and the Koran are yet another move by Satan in his aggressive quest to distract mankind from the essence of Christ and God's redemption plan. Any teaching that undermines the essence of Jesus' divinity, His death, and resurrection is simply satanic and anti-Christ. The Koran does exactly that:

• **According to the teachings of many Muslim clerics, it was Judas [not Jesus] that was crucified. So the Koran portrays the Crucifixion of Jesus as a scam:**

That they said, "we killed Christ Jesus the son of Mary, the Messenger of Allah"; - but they did not kill him, nor cruci-

fied him, but so it was made to appear to them, and those who differ therein are full of doubts, with no knowledge, but only conjecture to follow, but of a surety they did not kill him -- SURAH 4:157.

• **Islam denies the Deity of Jesus Christ; curses those who confess Him as the Son of God:**

The Jews call Uzair a son of Allah, and the Christians call Christ the Son of Allah... Allah's curse be upon them: how they are deluded away from the truth! -- SURAH 9:30

• **Islam portrays Jesus simply as a prophet:**

Christ the son of Mary was no more than a Messenger; many were the Messengers that passed away before him. His mother was a woman of truth. They had both to eat their (daily) food. See how Allah makes His signs clear to them; yet see in what ways they are deluded away from the truth -- SURAH 5:75.

Satan knows that Jesus Christ is the **centerpiece of God's Salvation plan** for you; and if he can get you to reject Jesus, he's got you going to hell with him. This is the reason why Christians all over the world must fervently pray for our Muslim brothers and sisters to be saved from this grand satanic deception called Islam, the false prophet called Mohammed, and the idol called Allah.

The Koran, therefore, was written by divination, and not by inspiration. Therefore, it is not the word of God. The Holy Bible, on the other hand, was written by divine inspiration.

The Bible is a divine revelation written by men as the Holy Spirit inspired them:

> 2Timothy 3:16 *All scripture is given by **inspiration of God**, and is profitable for doctrine, for reproof, for correction, for instruction in righteousness.*

According the *Strong* Dictionary, the phrase "inspiration of God" came from a Greek word "theopneustos" (theh-op'-nyoo-stos) meaning divinely breathed in: a message given by inspiration of God. The word **"Inspiration"** means impartation of an idea, encouragement, or motivation to do something.

::CHAPTER SIXTEEN

INSPIRATION
VERSUS
DIVINATION

The 66 books that comprise the Holy Bible have such unsurpassed harmony in covering thousands of years of human history. Written by men **inspired by God** over a period estimated to be about 1500 years, **these men were never out of their bodies or minds as they wrote down the inspired words. They were actively engaged [body, mind, and spirit] in the process.** They were physically and mentally conscious, with all their personal moral judgment, thoughts, attitudes, perceptions and conscience involved throughout the process of seeing, hearing, and writing the word of God. Where they were not sure what God wanted them to say or write, they asked Him for clarity. They physically and mentally, consciously and conscientiously, used their native languages, words, phrases and texts to convey the divine message. They were mentally conscious and their spirits were subject to their control throughout the process. This type of meditation is scriptural:

> **1 Corinthians 14:32** *And the spirits of the prophets are subject to the prophets.*

Unlike Mohammed's automatic writing/dictation, these individuals did not write against their conscience, will or belief. In fact, they argued and asked questions in many instances when their human minds could not comprehend the Wisdom of the Almighty God. The Koran is a complete contradiction to the Holy Bible. God gave us the Holy Bible to guide us to the right path. Then

Satan invented the Koran to throw us off-course. Satan is a trickster who preys on the ignorant. You become **ignorant when you disregard the truth.** Satan will use everything at his disposal to get you to ignore the truth and get you busy with religion, until it is too late.

So how would you know if the spirit attributed to your worship is God? The answer is in 1John 4:1-3 and 1Corinthians 14:29:

> **1John 4:2-3** *By this you know the Spirit of God: every spirit which confesses that Jesus Christ has come in the flesh is of God, and every spirit which does not confess Jesus is not of God. This is the spirit of Antichrist, of which you heard that it was coming, and now it is in the world already.*

> **1Corinthians 14:29** *Let the prophets speak two or three, and let the other judge.*

Every prophet, prophecy, revelation or word must be tested or judged by the Word of God: *if it denies Jesus Christ as the Son of God, and if it denies Jesus' death and resurrection, then it is not of the Spirit of God; it is not scriptural, it is of the antichrist spirit.*

The spirit that spoke with Mohammed does not pass this test. So the spirit of Islam is the spirit of the Antichrist.

:: RELIGIONIZING THE ONE TRUE FAITH

Today, as the Faith in Jesus Christ has been grossly religionized and institutionalized, it becomes vitally important for anyone who professes to be a Christian to test every activity in the Church by the Word of God. Why? Because religious idolatry has infiltrated the Church; and many innocent people are confused because many things that are not faith are now taught as faith. Scripture commands that we flee from religion as it appears to be godly but it lacks God's righteous life-transforming, life-giving, and life-saving Power:

> **2Timothy 3:5** ... *Having a form of godliness [religious appearance], but denying the power [life of God] thereof: from such turn away.*

So if scripture says to turn away from religion/religious people, to whom/what should we then turn? Know for sure that your redemption is not in status-quo Christianity, Islam, Buddhism, or any other. Your redemption is in Jesus Christ the Son of the Living God. The covenant promise God made to Abraham was that He will make of him a great nation, and the great nation shall possess many nations. Thus Abraham shall become father of many nations. I announce to you that the covenant promise is a generational peace/prosperity extending beyond the life-time of Abraham to the hereafter:

Genesis 12:2 *And I will make of thee a great nation.*

Genesis 17:4 *As for me, behold, my covenant is with thee, and thou shalt be a father of many nations.*

Genesis 17:7 *And I will establish my covenant between me and thee and thy seed after thee in their generations for an everlasting covenant, to be a God unto thee, and to thy seed after thee.*

Genesis 17:8 *And I will give unto thee, and to thy seed after thee, the land wherein thou art a stranger, all the land of Canaan, for an everlasting possession; and I will be their God.*

Now if you understand that the Isaac that was to be slain prophetically pointed to the Jesus that was slain on Calvary, then you'd understand that the great nation which God made out of *the womb* of Abraham is not just the Jews but also the number of Gentiles who choose to believe in Jesus. Now it is through Jesus' reconciliation Body that all *governments, businesses, and civic communities* hitherto cursed (separated from God) shall now be blessed (reconciled to God) (Colossians 1:20). Jesus' last instruction to His body is to reach-out to the cursed (the unsaved) in the power of His love that they may come to His saving knowledge and be rescued from the unprecedented terror that lies ahead.

Such will be God's agents of change and transformation anointed to reach-out to the lost *Muslims, Buddhists, Hypnotists, Satanists, New-Agers, Jews, Gentiles, and terrorists* of all ages including Osama bin Laden and his coalition, as well as lost *Christians.* Yes, many who call themselves Christians are today lost in the deception of religion, humanism, and false doctrines; so they need to be reached-out to.

:: JESUS COMING BACK SOON

Jesus is coming back soon, to take His Church to Heaven. Those left behind will experience a great tribulation for their refusal to believe in Jesus the Son of God. No one knows exactly when this will happen but there are biblical indications that we are very close to that hour. Thus the biblical experience I have shared with you in the first chapter of this book. I have also shared many other signs that the Lord has given to me that you may know the season and time in which we now live. Many will call these signs *speculations*, but I'm sure many more people will be saved by them. According to **Proverbs 20:8**, a true leader of a household, city or nation must be a visionary, who, not only is able to perceive trouble from afar, but is also able to take appropriate actions to avert or prevail over the trouble. You may not be able to stop this disaster from happening, but you sure can make adequate preparation to limit its consequences in your life and nation. Please act now before it is too late.

::CHAPTER SEVENTEEN

RELIGION,
A THREAT TO LIBERTY

According to Webster's Collegiate Dictionary 10th Edition, freedom is liberation from slavery or restraint; liberation from the power of another.

The Bible says, it is for freedom (liberty) that Christ has set us free; no longer to be subject to religious slavery:

> **Galatians 5:1** *For freedom Christ has set us free; stand fast therefore, and do not submit again to a yoke of slavery.*

To be truly free or liberated, not only must you be set free from a power that hitherto kept you in bondage, you must also be sustained in your freedom by the power that set you free; lest you go back into bondage. The restraint to keep you from falling back into bondage is the law of the *Spirit of life:* for there is therefore now no condemnation to them which are in Christ Jesus, who walk not after the flesh, but after the Spirit. For **the law of the Spirit of life in Christ Jesus** hath made me [them] free from **the law of sin and death** (Romans 8:1-2).

:: THE LAW OF FREEDOM

There is no freedom without obligation to the law of the Spirit of freedom. To be free from captivity is to be obligated to the law of the Spirit of Freedom; for where the Spirit of God is, there is liberty. Freedom then becomes a gift, or better still, a privilege that invariably vanishes in the absence of a continued obligation to the Spirit of life. The Spirit of life does come with guidance for righteous living, for where there is no godly guidance, the people fall back into sin and go back into bondage. But godly guidance or righteous leadership guarantees safety and protection from snares:

> **Proverbs 11:14** *Where no counsel is, the people fall: but in the multitude of counselors* **there** *is safety.*

> **Proverbs 29:18** *Where there is no vision, the people perish: but he that keepeth the law, happy* **is** *he.*

Where there is a lack of godly perspective, righteous insight/discipline, people soon forfeit the necessary protection or safety that the law of life brings. But with obedience to the law comes blessings, not curses. Therefore freedom without obligation to the law leads to nothing but foolishness and rebellion. That is why the fool says in his heart, there is no God; he believes he is not obligated to God's higher power and his life is in his hand. Therefore he casts off all restraints, and lives life without accountability to God:

> **Psalm 14:1-5** *The fool says in his heart, "There is no God." They are corrupt, they do abominable deeds, there is none that does good. The LORD looks down from heaven upon the children of men, to see if there are any that act wisely, that seek after God. They have*

*all gone astray, they are all alike corrupt; there is none that does good, no, not one. Have they no knowledge, all the evildoers who eat up my people as they eat bread, and do not call upon the LORD? There they shall be in **great terror**, for God is with the generation of the righteous."*

Interestingly, this scripture promises a great deal of terror [horror, bondage] for him who forsakes God [and His righteous laws]. It promises that God will be with the righteous, but will forsake the unrighteous (the lawless).

Now I said all that to say this: the blessing of liberty that we so much enjoy in America comes via a corresponding law- the law of the Spirit of life- that has the potency to keep us from bondage. Extricating ourselves from this law will only amount to forfeiture of the blessings that it brings. I will explain myself in a moment.

:: LIBERTY IN THE NATIONS (THE ISRAEL EXAMPLE)

For the Israelites to understand and appreciate the essence of freedom and the worth of liberty, God caused them to experience severe bondage in the hands of the Egyptians before allowing them to have a taste of the blessing of Liberty as they headed out towards the Promised Land. Spelling out the terms of freedom to them, Moses states:

Deuteronomy 11:26-28 *Behold, I set before you this day a blessing and a curse: the blessing, if you obey the commandments of the LORD your God, which I command you this day, and the curse, if you do not obey the commandments of the LORD your God, but turn aside from the way which I command you this day, to go after other gods which you have not known.*

In other words, for Israel to keep enjoying the prosperity/freedom, it had to adhere to God's rules/regulations:

Deuteronomy 11:13-14 *And if you will obey my commandments which I command you this day, to love the LORD your God, and to serve him with all your heart and with all your soul, he [God] will give the rain for your land in its season, the early rain and the later rain, that you may gather in your grain and your wine and your oil.*

Moses made it clear that their disobedience to God's righteous law would only bring about their downfall:

Deuteronomy 11:16-17 *Take heed lest your heart be deceived, and you turn aside and serve other gods and worship them, and the anger of the LORD be kindled against you, and he [God] shut up the heavens, so that there be no rain, and the land yield no fruit, and you perish quickly off the good land which the LORD gives you.*

It follows that a nation that desires to come out from under a curse to enjoy the blessing of liberty must follow the Lord's commands. Let me use yet another nation to explain this principle here.

:: THE CASE OF HAITI

The nation of Haiti is a good case in point here: Statistics on Haiti culled from USA **Today** *March 2, 2004 page 2A* shows that:

- Less than 70% of Haiti's children are receiving a primary education.
- Roughly 12% of children born in Haiti die before the age of 5.
- Only 1/4 of the population has access to safe drinking water.
- Adult Haitians don't live long- life expectancy is barely 52 years.
- HIV rate is high- about 6.1% in 2001.
- Half the population publicly practice Voodoo.
- About 80% of the 7.5 million populations live in abject poverty.
- Only about 53% of adults can read/write.
- The country is said to be about the size of Maryland, but there are very few highways; very few roads are paved: 1,957 miles unpaved, 628 paved.

It you think it is geographical location that brings blessings to a nation, think again. Ask yourself why Haiti was so cursed while its next-door neighbor, the Dominican Republic, has been relatively prosperous: *blessed with green grass and good fruit.* The nation of Haiti is just now recovering from centuries of devastation only because hundreds of thousands of Christians came together in prayer to disrupt the nation's 200 year-old diabolical blood pact with the devil. Prior to that, ousted President Aristide had passed a law recognizing voodoo as a valid Haitian religion. August. 14, 2003 was scheduled to be the day to ratify the 200-year-old voodoo pact, for which purpose the now exiled Aristide had flown in over 400 voodoo practitioners from all over the world. But for the prayers of Christians who were truly pro-active to break that curse and actively avert the demonic plot, that satanic covenant would have been renewed; and only God knows how devastated Haiti would have been by now. Now let me relate this principle to America.

:: FREEDOM PERVERTED IN AMERICA

God's law that applied to Israel and Haiti is no different from that which applied to *Adam and Eve.* The Almighty God does not give freedom and liberty without obligation to His Spirit who guarantees us freedom. The moment Adam and Eve rejected the Law of the Spirit of Liberty, they ate the forbidden fruit; and the rest is history. Now if God's standard holds true for Adam and

Eve, Israel, and Haiti, it definitely holds true for America. It seems to me that majority of the present generation of Americans do not know the source of their blessing of liberty; and so they are oblivious of what it takes to sustain it:

> **Judges 2:10** *And also all that generation were gathered unto their fathers: and there arose **another generation [of Americans]** after them, which knew not the LORD, nor yet the works which he had done for Israel [**America**]. And the children of Israel [this new generation of Americans] did evil in the sight of the LORD, and served Baalim (idols) [**yielded to immorality and all sorts of sin**].*

Freedom becomes perverted when a nation goes from one generation to another without making conscious efforts to pass on the knowledge of the Lord God. As part of our obligation to the covenant, we are to pass on the knowledge of the Lord God to our children and children's children; and put in place monuments, structures, and moral laws to keep us in check, so we don't take our freedom for granted and depart from the Lord. America has certainly taken its freedom for granted. Some lawmakers would rather let the citizens live and die in sin than to confront the tough issues of sin and immorality in our society. They would rather you (the citizens) live without God in your lives than to lose your precious votes.

:: "NO OBLIGATION" TYPE FREEDOM

It is dangerous for a nation to define freedom from the standpoint of *"no obligation to God"*. Freedom is not the lack of restriction so that you can do whatever you want. Freedom is the liberty to be everything that God wants you to be. It is the God of Abraham, Isaac, and Jacob that has blessed America; and that is not without obligation to His law of the Spirit of freedom.

Liberty is not freedom to serve sin; it is freedom to serve God. For America to be a true instrument of liberty in Iraq, Afghanistan, and other places, America must propagate righteousness and forsake politically correct ideologies that contradict God's holy principles. I don't know about others, but in the Southern part of Nigeria, America is usually referred to as *God's Own Country.* This is because it is quite obvious to us in that part of the world that it is impossible for any nation to enjoy this much prosperity and protection like America has enjoyed except by the favor of the Almighty God. Believe it or not, only a covenant people prospers the way America has prospered among the nations of the world. Covenant people have an agreement or contract with the Lord: that He will be their God and they will be His people (Genesis 17:4, 7, 8). A primary term of the covenant will be for the people to live and conduct their daily lives to honor God. Then God, in return, will shower them with favor to the envy of other nations.

::CHAPTER EIGHTEEN

AMERICA'S LIVING CONSTITUTION DICHOTOMY

Like Israel, especially under King Solomon, America is one nation that has experienced such great favor in the sight of God.

America's covenant with God was undeniably documented as the Constitution establishing the United States of America and the States within the Republic. Just as the Holy Bible is the sacred document that guides us in our covenant relationship with God, the American Constitution is a sacred document born out of a covenant relationship with God. Signed on September 17, 1787 by a group of faithful Christians, the document was meant to guide the nation in its covenant relationship with God. But unlike the Bible- *regarded as the living word*- for which reason perverting it is forbidden (Revelation 22:18), the American Constitution is also regarded by many as *a living Constitution* but, sadly, for a reason other than to preserve its integrity. Ordinarily, you would expect the American Constitution to still mean what it meant at the time it was signed. **Unfortunately, out of sheer disregard for God, a faction of the society- the Church and State separatists- advocate that the Constitution means whatever they want it to mean at the time they want it to mean whatever they want it to mean.**

Sadly, this living Constitution dichotomy was only to weaken America's spiritual heritage, treating with contempt the nation's covenant relationship with God. Today, part of the American Constitution is now portrayed to mean different things at different times depending on individual social/political preferences, religious persuasions, and personal indulgences. To me this concept is simply an open-door strategy to remove God's name from America and allow for further secularization of this great nation. In my opinion, America's Constitution should have been treated with much respect and its integrity preserved in order to uphold the nation's Christian values and heritage; if anything, to keep the flow of the blessing of liberty.

What makes a nation great is not its military prowess, economic power, or scientific advancement. It is God's favor that brings both spiritual and material blessings to a nation. The story should be told again and again of the nation's founding fathers who sought the liberty to worship God in spirit and truth as a result of which America was founded on the basis of the Christian faith.

:: A BROKEN COVENANT

America has broken covenant with God by legitimizing pagan activities and normalizing immorality on the ground of tolerance and civility. Please understand that Civility is no ground for Immorality. You cannot use love to justify sinful practices, for God is love; neither can you use liberty, for God is its giver.

Breaking covenant with God has far-reaching consequences. Americans, as a people, have enjoyed much liberty like no other because God wanted America to set a good economic, moral, and spiritual standard for the rest of the world to emulate. Unfortunately America has defied God's authority by abusing liberty and misrepresenting love.

It is a blatant affront for a nation to make laws that defy God's authority. We all must understand that **the God of Liberty is the God of Justice and the God of Righteousness**. I suggest therefore that Americans, individually and corporately, repent and return to God, bearing in mind that our God is a merciful God. He will forgive if we humble ourselves and truly ask for forgiveness.

The same goes for the rest of the nations of the world. We all have breached agreement with our creator. We have all gone astray by worshipping other gods especially where cultures and traditions are concerned. Many nations, including Nigeria, are guilty in this regard. Because we have placed ungodly cultures and traditions above God's principles, we are guilty of violating the very first commandment of God [Exodus 20:4-5] in hundreds of conspicuous and inconspicuous ways:

> **Exodus 20:4-5** *Thou shalt not make unto thee **any graven image, or any likeness of any thing** that is in heaven above, or that is in the earth beneath, or that*

*is in the water under the earth: Thou shalt **not bow down thyself to them**, nor serve them: for I the LORD thy God am a jealous God, visiting the iniquity of the fathers upon the children unto the third and fourth generation of them that hate me...*

But there is forgiveness for the guilty.

:: FORGIVENESS FOR THE GUILTY

The absence of guilty feelings does not mean the lack of guilt because many consciences have become seared. Whether we feel guilty or not, Sin makes us automatically guilty before a Holy God, and makes us vulnerable to the adversary. Sin and guilt come when we fail to do what God expects or demands as a standard for living. But Christ frees us from the power of sin and condemnation not by excusing our sins, but by empowering us to defeat sin in our lives. The fact is, the whole nations of the earth are on death row; and without Jesus none of us have any hope.

As nations, we are to corporately put our confidence in Jesus Christ to take away our sins and remove our guilt so God can heal our lands (2Chronicles 7:14). We are declared "not guilty" only if we ask Jesus to cleanse our lands with His blood.

:: NIGERIA GUILTY

In a number of ways, Nigeria, as a nation, is guilty of the sin of idolatry as you find people from all walks of life participating in direct and indirect worship of hundreds of idols made from woods, stones, water, air, and iron. There is no doubt that iniquities of social injustice, poverty, disease, sickness, crime, immorality, and all manner of evil have continued to flow from one generation to the next because of idolatry. The situation has become even more complicated because majority of Nigeria's purported sixty-something million Christians, who are supposed to know better, are themselves caught up in the web of ungodly traditions and cultures that violate God's commandment.

Many people think it is God who gave them their traditions and customs to practice, but that is not true. God is not a hypocrite: He will not give you what will kill you and then blame you for it.

:: RELIGIONS AND TRADITIONS

Religions, as well as ungodly traditions and customs, all take their roots from old pagan practices, myths, and superstitions cleverly orchestrated by Satan. However, the Holy Bible is given so that none will be ignorant of the truth (Leviticus 26:1; Exodus 20:4-5; Exodus 23:24; Deuteronomy 5:9; Psalm 95:6).

Many nations, out of ignorance, have entered into covenants with Satan. Thus they have opened their doors to ravaging spirits and have exposed their people to social injustice, political chaos, and economic wretchedness. For instance, the leaders of the nation of Haiti were said to have pledged allegiance to Satan in return for "freedom" from the French imperialists. What did they gain in return? *Unparalleled poverty!* Today, Haiti is pretty much the poorest nation on earth.

In 1996, Nigeria's ousted military dictator Ibrahim Babangida ignorantly engaged Nigeria in an ungodly covenant with the Organization of Islamic Conference- OIC. As a result, Nigeria's ailing economy fast plummeted to a worst level. Much devastation had come upon Nigeria's Oil Industry since then. As at the time of compiling information for this book, only one of Nigeria's four State-run refineries was in operation, way below capacity. **This has forced Nigeria to become a gasoline-importing nation. What a mockery!**

Today, many Nigerians are living in "hell" as the price of gasoline continues to soar way beyond their income. Many lives have been lost in riots and many homes destroyed as a result of explosions caused by impure gasoline sold in the country. But for the prayers of Christians, Nigeria would probably have been involved in one of the bloodiest civil wars in man's history. That probably would have plunged the nation into an irreversible desolation worst than the Rwanda genocide that destroyed well over 860,000 lives.

Please understand that I am not trying to knock anybody or pick on my Muslim brothers and sisters; I only want you to know that according to God's covenant promise, only the seed of Abraham- Jesus Christ and His generations (Matthew 1:1) have the power to break the Curse over the nations and heal the land (Genesis 12:3).

I welcome anyone, from any part of the country to serve in any leadership capacity in Nigeria as the Lord would allow; but there is a vital need for every leader to be born-again and be filled with the Holy Spirit for such is *the seed of Abraham* empowered to break the curse and lead the nation from despair to joy. God has made so many great promises concerning Nigeria, but these are covenant promises hinged on covenant requirements that can only be fulfilled through God's covenant children.

:: UNPRECEDENTED ELECTIONS

Recently the Lord told me that **the unprecedented** will happen in Nigeria and America. God wants to transform Nigeria. The Lord impressed it upon my heart that there is a serious leadership vacuum in Nigeria. I believe that the next Presidential Elections in Nigeria (2011) and In America (2008) will be truly unprecedented.

Indeed, in a vision, I saw a line-up of the 2008 United States Presidential candidates. I saw Senator Barak Obama step out of the shadows (very significant in meaning). Now whether the Lord will turn that into a White House victory for him, I do not know yet. But one thing is for sure, the U.S. 2008 Presidential Election will be unprecedented.

With regards to Nigeria, many **questions arise as to who will lead Nigerians from the current state of despair to the future state of joy:**

- Will the Body of Christ rise up to the task?
- Will the Body of Christ be united and bold enough to start a **non-violent** political, social, and economic revolution in Nigeria?
- Will the Saints of the Most High God rise up to the demands of this crucial time to dislodge *the enemies of righteousness* in order to establish godliness in Nigeria?

These are some of the real questions demanding real answers at this time.

::CHAPTER NINETEEN

PLURALISM

///////⊛///////

Pluralism, a condition of being multiple or plural, is defined by The American Heritage Dictionary as a condition in which numerous distinct ethnic, religious, or cultural groups are present and tolerated within a society.

Pluralism is especially favored in European and Western societies where slavery (involuntary servitude) was legitimized and used extensively to facilitate economic growth. On the face value, Pluralism appears to be an ideal concept even as you consider a nation like America that has benefited tremendously from the raw labor and expertise of people of diverse ethnic, religious, or cultural, and national backgrounds.

However, my focus in this chapter is on religious pluralism, also known as Syncretism. Syncretism, according to the American Heritage Dictionary, is the reconciliation or fusion of differing systems of belief, as in philosophy or religion. Religion is probably the most controversial topic on planet earth right now. But bizarre is the attempt to harmonize religions with a view to solving societal problems. This idea is called Syncretism.

Religious pluralism is the folly of pursuing a "peaceful" co-existence of philosophies, ideas, beliefs, practices, cultures, notions, opinions, etc, as a basis for generating a view or belief that satisfies the generality of the world but opposes biblical truth.

The momentary peace syncretism offers is a false peace because it is not the Peace of God, and does not bring about Peace with God. I suggest to you that the peace that Pope Benedict VI is trying to forge between Christians and Muslims and Jews is needful but will not last.

:: ONE NATION-ONE GOD?

As a *One Nation-One God* people, America enjoyed what is a goodly heritage that caused God's Blessings to abound in the nation. The Blessing then attracted many people from other nations, catalyzing immigration of millions from other nations, cultures, traditions and religious background. Plus, millions of people from other parts of the world who fled their native repressive environments in search of *the American dream, which, essentially, is the freedom, liberty, and prosperity that the God of Abraham, Isaac, and Jacob bestowed on the nation because of its allegiance to Jesus the Son of the Living God.* This, in addition to the phenomenal increase in immigration from the Orient and the Middle East after the Second World War is what essentially made America the melting-pot of nations. Most immigrants came in with their ungodly traditions, cultures, and religions; and in no time, they began to seek religious rights as well as ethnic and racial recognitions. Sadly, America did not only embrace these immigrants, it also embraced their idols and sinful practices. This marked the dawn of **religious pluralism** in America.

Little did America know that *Religious Pluralism is nothing but cohabitation with idols.* Now the nation has become spiritually apathetic. Although many claim to be Christians, they are only a few steps away from spiritual bankruptcy. Like the Israelites, the idolatry and other abominable practices that Americans decided to cohabitate with have now become a thorn in their flesh and a snare to their souls (Judges 2:1-5).

:: PLURALISM IS SPIRITUAL IDOLATRY

God loves us absolutely, but He has absolute **intolerance** for idolatry. A society that claims to love God must constantly purge itself of idolatry and guard against pagan infiltration. Instead of allowing its goodly heritage to be the bedrock of its local, national, and international policies, the nation embarked on a futile journey to propagate ideals contrary to its true spiritual foundation. The implications of being pluralistic are more far-reaching than you may ever imagine. In a pluralistic society such as America, standing in opposition against **popular and ungodly views** can sure make you unpopular especially when it seems as if everyone is in agreement except you. However, I assure you that it is more worthy to uphold God's principles than to go with the winds of ungodly public opinion.

Below are some of the lies pluralism wants you to believe to be true:

- Every religion is acceptable to God.
- We all worship the same God through many different avenues, methods or faiths.
- There are many gods as there are many faiths.
- Religions represent the many faiths and roads to God (and Heaven).
- You can choose any religion that suits your ego. All roads lead to God, anyway.

The most grievous implication of religious pluralism is the estrangement of Church and State, which is a whole different subject (by itself) that I cannot fully discuss in this book. Sadly, religion has also defiled the Church.

In a pluralistic society, the road to "salvation" is **wide**, and full of many options. Unfortunately, all of them lead to destruction. However, Jesus is the **narrow** path that leads to life. This leaves us with only one option: Jesus, and Jesus only.

> **John 14:6** *Jesus said to him, "I am the way, and the truth, and the life; no one comes to the Father, but by me.*

> **Matthew 7:13-15** *"Enter ye in at the strait gate: for wide is the gate, and broad is the way, that leadeth to destruction, and many there be which go in thereat: Because strait is the gate, and narrow is the way, which leadeth unto life, and few there be that find it. Beware*

of false prophets, which come to you in sheep's clothing, but inwardly they are ravening wolves."

Other Warnings about Religious Pluralism:

2 Peter 2:2 *And many shall follow their pernicious [destructive] ways; by reason of whom the way of truth shall be evil spoken of.*

2 Peter 2:15 *Which have forsaken the right way, and are gone astray, following the way of Balaam (a false prophet) the son of Bosor, who loved the wages of unrighteousness;*

2 Peter 2:21 *For it had been better for them not to have known the way of righteousness, than, after they have known it, to turn from the holy commandment delivered unto them.*

Jude 1:11 *Woe unto them! For they have gone in the way of Cain, and ran greedily after the error of Balaam for reward, and perished in the gainsaying of Core.*

:: DISCERNING RELIGIOUS DECEPTIONS

The world says every religion must be respected and treated equally. But God wants us to discern the spirits behind religions so we can appreciate the fact that true liberty comes not from religion but from the Christ

(2 Peter 2:19; 1John 4:1). Faith in God therefore is not a practice of religious cultures or traditions. Rather, it is the practice of sound biblical principles exhorted by Christ and His Prophets.

Furthermore, God sends physical signs (storms, tornadoes, earthquakes, etc) from heaven to alert us and remind us of our fragility. He also sends His Prophets, and has put forth many signs, but the nations have continued to ignore them. Returning to God will be a choice that America and the whole world will have to make.

:: CHURCH CONTAMINATED BY RELIGION

The Church in America has not made things any easier for the nation. **Many church leaders, in their zeal to show kinship between the true Christian faith and the world's religious belief systems, have harmonized their faith with many pagan ideologies.** In their eagerness to avoid controversies and be at "**peace**" with their pagan neighbors, many Christians have compromised God's commandments even as their church denominations and seminaries continue to spend millions of dollars yearly to promote "**mainstream theologies**" designed to appease the world. Essentially, this has rendered their gospel powerless, and of no effect.

The whole world today continuing to plummet into moral, spiritual, political, social and economic decadence is not unconnected with the sorry condition of the generality of the Church. The following statistics (culled from *World Magazine*, December 6, 2003, Page 33) speaks of the present unacceptable condition of the church in America:

- Most Christians think every religion is equal/valid
- 26% of born-again Christians believe that all religions are essentially the same
- 50% of born-again Christians believe that a life of good works will enable a person to get to heaven
- 35% of born-again Christians do not believe that Jesus Christ physically rose from the dead
- 52% do not believe that the Holy Spirit is a living entity. Slightly more born-again Christians believe in the devil than believe in the Holy Spirit
- 45% do not believe that Satan exists
- 10% believe in reincarnation and 20% believe it is possible to communicate with the dead
- 33% accepts same sex unions
- 39% believe it is morally acceptable for couples to live together before marriage. And significantly, born-again Christians are more likely than non-Christians to have experienced divorce.

The preceding statistics is a true reflection of the deplorable spiritual condition of the Church as well as the unbelievable level of ignorance in the American society. This, of course, tells you how much the Church has flirted with religion. This explains why America has become very secularized.

In warning us to be careful of *the way* of the Gentiles (Matthew 16:6;12), Jesus was in fact telling us to be **careful of the lifestyle of the dogs, outcasts, heathens, outsiders, unsaved, unbelievers.** He was instructing us to not allow foreign lifestyles (*forms, rules, regulations, idols, traditions, and religious practices*) to infiltrate the Church and contaminate the pure faith. Unfortunately that has now happened in America and certainly all over the nations of the world.

Certainly I am not advocating *Isolation* here. I am advocating *Separation*- total commitment to God Almighty through Jesus Christ only. I am not suggesting hatred towards our Muslim brothers and sisters and other non-Christians. Jesus demands that, we, His followers **relate to others in love; but we are not to compromise our faith.** True Christians are to love all people, but they are to diligently guard their hearts against social, economic, political, and religious defilement.

Today, Satan is using false definition of **love and peace** to get the true Christians to compromise their faith. Thus many are promoting false peace all over the world. Let it be known that there can be no lasting peace except by Jesus the Prince of Peace.

::CHAPTER TWENTY

INTRIGUES
OF
REDEMPTION

I cannot over-emphasize the fact that many people who have been grossly ravaged by hunger, disease, poverty, war, and terrorism are now crying out to God for restoration. The word "restoration" implies a return to an original state or ownership. Therefore restoration today would mean a world of peace, love, health, virtues, and surplus in the context of God our creator. But restoration will not happen unless we understand God's original intent for life on earth. Thus God's restoration strategy for today requires that we understand how things were originally, in the beginning; and why they are the way they are now.

:: GOD'S ORIGINAL INTENT

A majority of Bible-believing Christians will agree with me that God's plan for their lives dates as far back as the beginning, in which the LORD God created Adam and Eve, and entrusted them with the Vision to rule over the domain called *Earth*. The assignment was for them to bring forth a godly civilization comprising *entertainments, artifacts, military, science & technology, agriculture, relationships, governments, commerce, marriage, family, education systems, etc* to reflect the glory, honor, and power of God as the Supreme Ruler of the entire universe (Genesis 1:26-30).

Although God did not **relinquish** his Supreme Lordship over His creation, He delegated the government of this world to the man He created, meaning God intends to rule His creation through man- a concept widely known as **Theocracy**:

> **Isaiah 37:16** *O LORD of hosts, God of Israel, that dwellest **between** the Cherubims, thou **art** the God, even thou alone, of all the kingdoms of the earth: thou hast made heaven and earth.*

In the beginning, Adam and Eve (our forefathers) lived a perfect life in a perfect environment (Garden of Eden) until they allowed Sin into their lives; no thanks to Satan (Genesis 3; 4:18-22). As a result of their fall, mankind officially lost rulership authority to Satan. As mankind became more and more alienated from God, man's *vision* for civilization became more and more corrupted, reflecting evil rather than good (Genesis 6).

Meanwhile Satan continued to influence mankind with counterfeit deities (idols) fashioned along diverse *geophysical locations, languages, ideas, habits, diets, inclinations, beliefs and superstitions.* Thus the nations lost sight of the One true God, and took on a *many gods-many religions* stance.

Thus the world became filled with death instead of life; mortality instead of immortality; immorality instead of morality; violence instead of peace; evil instead of good; and curses instead of blessings. Instead of a world of peace, love, good health and godly values, mankind began to function primarily in a world of pains, sickness, diseases, immorality, and terror. In other words, the Kingdom of God suffered a huge setback (Matthew 11:12).

This decadence was fast played-out in Adam's first family as Cain (Adam's first son), out of rage, anger, and jealousy, murders his brother Abel (Genesis 4). That is why the scripture says that sin came into the world through Adam, and as result, **all of mankind became sinners, inheriting death instead of life:**

> **Romans 5:12** *Wherefore, as by one man [Adam] sin entered into the world, and death by sin; and so death passed upon all men for that all have sinned.*

Therefore, every person born of a woman on the face of the earth according to Adam is born spiritually dead and condemned for hell, no exception. But the Bible says that God is Love (1John 4:8). His Love motivated Him to create us, and His Love motivated Him to send us a Messiah to redeem us from the fall; for God so loved the world that He gave His only begotten Son, that whosoever believes in Him shall not perish but have everlasting life (John 3:16).

Now let us take a moment to examine the nature and gravity of the fall in order to better understand the nature and gravity of the redemption.

:: INTRIGUES OF REDEMPTION

Had God not provided us with a *blood covenant of mercy*, the entire human race would have been completely destroyed. **But why a blood covenant?** A blood covenant because life is synonymous with the blood. If you cut-off the blood supply, you cut-off the life. If you give the blood, you give the life:

> **Leviticus 17:11** *For the life of the flesh is in the blood: and I have given it to you upon the altar to make an atonement for your souls: for it is the blood that maketh an atonement for the soul.... For it is the life of all flesh; the blood of it is for the life thereof: ...for the life of all flesh is the blood thereof.*

Because *man committed* the offense, *man* would have to pay the penalty ultimately. But in the meantime, God, through the blood of innocent animals provided us with temporary life until the appointed time for the Messiah-Jesus (the perfect *Lamb)* to appear and provide us with permanent/everlasting life through His perfect blood.

By the time Jesus came into the world, the whole world was already entrenched in spiritual adultery (systems of religions, traditions, and cultures all orchestrated by Satan). In fact nations such as India still have as many as one million officially recognized gods. That is how despicable the Idolatry issue is.

Now specific violations of any one of God's commandments carry specific penalties. The specific sin of Adam and Eve carried the **death penalty**, of which God forewarned them saying:

> **Genesis 2:17** *But of the tree of the knowledge of good and evil you shall not eat, for in the day that you eat of it you shall die.*

Death, in this case, includes physical degradation, eternal separation from God, and an everlasting torment in the lake of fire (Revelation 19:20; 20:10-15). Therefore, a person not redeemed by Jesus the Messiah is spiritually dead; though he is physically alive, he remains condemned. His eternal punishment officially begins when he dies physically. His physical body then goes back to dust while his spirit [soul] heads for hell. In other words, if you die as a Muslim, Buddhist, or whatever religion you have, you will never see God; but you will suffer in the company of Satan and his demons in hell.

However, it is possible for a sinner to be redeemed and to escape hell fire if, perhaps, someone else pays the penalty for his sin. In other words, if an innocent man offers to die to atone for the sin of a sinner, the sinner will be released from the charges. Thus God's mercy prevailed in the behalf of mankind. Premised by His love, God found a way to satisfy your *death penalty* by sending Jesus to die for your sin to free you from the curse of sin.

The bottom-line of Salvation is that God provided us with an innocent man- Jesus the Sacrificial Lamb of God- who would not only die to break the curse and satisfy the death penalty, but would also rise from the dead to lead His forgiven brothers and sisters back to their Father, their God:

> **Romans 5:18** *Therefore as by the offense of one judgment came upon all men to condemnation; even so by the righteousness of one the free gift came upon all men unto justification of life.*

> **Isaiah 53:5** *But He was wounded for our transgressions, he was bruised for our iniquities: the chastisement of our peace was upon him; and with his stripes we are healed.*

:: JESUS- THE WORD OF GOD

Now if God is God, which we know He is; how come He has a Son who is also God? Does that mean we have two Gods? The answer is No, there are not many Gods. There is only one God. God's Word and His Spirit are no different from God himself. The Word of God is pre-Bible and pre-biblical History. In error, we often see the Word of God through chronological time and seasons, hence we fail to appreciate His eternal nature. All scriptural principles demonstrated, spoken, and written in the Bible from Genesis to Revelation are pre-Genesis,

existing as part of the nature and character of God long before He created the world. Now being eternal and existing before the world began, the living Word is Jesus-an active person in whom the fullness of God dwells.

When God the Father created the world in the Spirit (Genesis 1), Jesus the Lord God translated Creation into the Physical state (Genesis 2; John 1). At the time appointed by God the Father, Jesus *the Word* became flesh and came to earth to save His creation (John 1:1-14; Colossians 1:15-19, Hebrews 4:12); the creation that was hijacked from Adam and Eve by Satan (Luke 4:5-8).

And so Jesus on earth was none other than God in human flesh:

> **Hebrews 10:5** *Consequently, when Christ came into the world, he said, Sacrifices and offerings thou hast not desired, but a **body** [flesh] hast thou prepared for me.*

> **1John 2:2** *And He [Jesus] is the propitiation [atonement, expiation, reconciliation, satisfaction] for our sins: and not for ours only, but also for **the sins** of the whole world.*

The human flesh is simply an earth-suit- the human body that clothes the spirit/soul. The earth-suit does not live forever; it goes back to dust when we die. It is our spirit/soul that lives forever. But we have to determine where we live. We have a choice of heaven or hell. To everyone is given the same opportunity to choose life or death. The message of the Gospel is to let everyone know that God has made for us a way of escape from eternal damnation. That way is Jesus Christ of Nazareth.

But there is one important condition: Salvation is not Automatic: If you wish to be redeemed by Jesus, you have to personally acknowledge your sin and guilt, and then receive salvation as a gift from God; not as anything you could ever earn through any works of *charities, mystics, philosophies, religions, and religious sacrifices of man, goats, rams, birds, or any other.*

In essence, Jesus died:

- To restore you and me into a loving relationship with God; no more alienation from God, and no more religious burdens. The breach between us sinners and a Holy God was mended by Christ's crucifixion, for God was in Christ reconciling the world to Himself (2 Corinthians 5:19).

- To restore the power and authority that we lost to Satan so that we can regain control of civilization and bring it under the rulership of God Almighty, just as it was in the beginning.

- To destroy the devil's ability to keep us in mental, spiritual, and physical bondage [Hebrews 2:14].

- To release us from the bondage of religion and free us from the problem of trying to obey God's good laws in our own failing strength [Colossians 2:14].

- To demonstrate the full extent of God's love for all-*Hispanics, English, Indians. Africans, Arabs, Americans, and everyone else* regardless of race, color, gender, profession, religious errors, and place of origin even while we were yet sinners [Romans 5:8].

So we see that God will not only save us from eternal damnation, He will also save us for eternal blessings.

:: HIGHWAY TO DESTINY

With Jesus in the lead, you can now go freely to fulfill your destiny as God originally intended:

> **Matthew 11:12** *And from the days of John the Baptist until now the kingdom of heaven suffereth violence, and the violent take it by force.*

This scripture is not talking about being violent; it is referring to the Generation of Jesus Christ empowered by the Holy Spirit to bring about change and transformation in this chaotic world. This is all about **Restoration:**

taking back all the kingdoms that the devil stole from us. And from the time of the Prophets of Old, even John the Baptist, there had been serious chaos in the world and serious setback in the affairs of the kingdom of God. However, Jesus has now established His Generation to restore order in the social, economic, and political arenas according to God's promise to Abraham, and Isaac and Jacob. The gathering of Jesus Christ's generations is called the Church and we are to propagate this message of restoration simply to restore the *Lost* back to God.

:: THE WORLD IN CONFLICT WITH THE CHURCH

The problem is, a lot of people want restoration, but they don't want to have anything to do with the Church. The world does rebuff the Church because we church-folks (so-called Christians) are sometimes very nasty, unreliable, judgmental, and hypocritical because of our own unresolved issues. However, I assure you that this message of Salvation is the truth regardless of the personal conducts and misconducts of any man or woman.

Besides, God is currently overhauling His Church, taking *her* through an unprecedented reformation to bring forth one that truly reflects God's image and likeness. While I encourage you to please look beyond the preacher and harken to Jesus the perfect one, I also encourage preachers to please understand that we are called to preach Jesus crucified, not ourselves. We must not religionize the message: We are to keep it real, pure, and simple.

I have also observed that many people want to be restored, but they assume they do not need Jesus to do that. **In fact many of my Muslim brothers and sisters contend that they do not need Jesus' mediation to be reconciled to God; more like accepting the gift and rejecting the giver:**

> **Act 4:12** *And there is salvation in no one else [except Jesus Christ of Nazareth], for there is no other name under heaven given among men by which we must be saved.*"

Yes you do need Jesus' mediation. Symbolized by the cross that saved me from hell, it was Jesus that saved me from hell as I headed down that valley of destruction at the age of 22. I assure you that your Salvation is in Jesus Christ alone; not in Mohammed, Buddha, Confucius, Shinto, Pope, Holy Mary, or Dalai Lama.

::CHAPTER TWENTY-ONE

SUPREMACY
OF
JESUS CHRIST

:: JESUS THE LAST ADAM

In Matthew 1:1, we see God start a new generation, the Jesus Generation, with its root not in Adam and Eve, but in Abraham and David. Why would God start a new generation of people?

By Genesis chapter 6, all humans (except Noah) were totally sold out to evil. Hence God wiped them all out in the flood, and started a new Family with Noah. But by the time of Genesis 12 (after Noah had died), all humans (except Abraham) were again completely sold out to evil. All had completely departed from righteousness and none, whatsoever, worshipped God. With the whole world lost to sin and death, God had to start a new Family- a new generation prophesied by God in Genesis 3:15-16 and materialized in Abraham, Isaac, and Jacob. The family became Israel, and out of Israel came Jesus the Messiah. Out of Jesus is born the righteous generation- the Church- that worship God, and not idols.

Now if Jesus had come in the lineage of the first Adam and Eve, He would have shared in their genetic proficiency [heredity] to sin. He would have been no different from you and me. As the Messiah, He had to bypass generational sins and genetic proficiency to sin that those who believe in Him will inherit [not sin and death as they did from the first Adam] but life everlasting, Amen. Thus Jesus is the last Adam; there is none after Him.

:: GENETIC ENGINEERING/MANIPULATION

I am not suggesting that God engaged in genetic engineering to remove all traits of sin and death from Jesus' DNA after He was formed in His mother's womb. I am saying that the Holy Spirit supernaturally implanted Mary's **virgin womb** with a **Holy Zygote** [the pure **seed** prophesied in Genesis 3:15 thousands of years earlier] to bring forth Jesus- **the last Adam.** In other words, to bring forth the man Jesus, God neither utilized a spermatozoon [sperm] from Joseph (Jesus' earthly father) nor relied on an ovum [egg] from Mary (Jesus' earthly mother). That is why Jesus, though fully human, did not carry any traits of sin or death in His spiritual genome; unlike you, me and all the world's religious figures like Mohammed, Buddha, Confucius, etc.

:: SUPERNATURAL PREGNANCY

The biblical account is that Mary, baffled by the prophecy of a pregnancy without sexual intercourse, specifically asked the angel Gabriel how the promise would come to pass since she was a virgin, and not yet married:

> **Luke 1:34-35** *And Mary said to the angel, "How shall this be, since I have no husband?" And the angel said to her, "The Holy Spirit will come upon you, and the power of the Most High will overshadow you; therefore the child to be born will be called holy, the Son of God.*

The word "Overshadow" is derived from the original Greek word episki-azo (ep-ee-skee-ad'-zo), meaning to envelop in a haze of brilliancy, clothed with Sun, or extraordinary influence. In essence, this is what the angel was saying to Mary:

God, your creator, is very familiar with your spiritual, physical, anatomical and physiological condition: He knows that you are a virgin, but He will envelope you in the brilliance of His glory and will supernaturally implant a Holy Zygote into your virgin womb. And because no man can take any credit for the pregnancy, the baby will have a unique identity as the Son of God. Therefore Jesus was the grand design of God.

:: THE IDENTITY OF JESUS

It is extremely important that I touch on this subject because the identity of Jesus is the **bone of contention** for many religious people, especially Muslims. They argue that God is too holy to have a son. But the truth is they are viewing the whole issue from a carnal standpoint. God did not bear Jesus like mere men bear children. He bore Him supernaturally, though He utilized Mary's virgin womb. The mystery here according to the prophecy is that a virgin will conceive and bear a son- **an unmistakable supernatural signal by which God would catch our attention, arouse our curiosity, and cause us to seek Him in truth:**

> **Isaiah 7:14** *Therefore the Lord himself shall give you a sign; Behold, a virgin shall conceive, and bear a son, and shall call his name **Emmanuel.***

This prophecy was given hundreds of years before Jesus was born. The virgin birth was designed to be a great sign, not a subject of debate or argument.

The name Emmanuel literally means **"with us is God"**. This is the good news, ladies and gentlemen; you don't need religion to get to God; for God is now in our midst. Religions today are nothing but modernized paganism and new age humanism. But I have good news for my fellow brothers and sisters in the religious world: **Don't look any further; God is now in our midst in the person of Jesus Christ.**

Even the religious people of Jesus' day had the same problem understanding, or should I say, believing this great wisdom of God. Although many of them under-stood and respected the fact that Jesus exhibited the su-pernatural, they had an issue with His identity as *the Son of God*. They could not even bear to hear Him referred to as such.

You see, to recognize and accept Jesus' unique identity will be to acknowledge that He is God. Remember, most of the religious people of Jesus' day saw Him grow up as a little boy in a carpenter's shed. So to them Jesus was just a mere son of a mere carpenter. Likewise, many of us, before accepting Christ, also reasoned like that.

:: ROYALTY OF JESUS PROPHESIED

In order to forestall all kinds of argument and confusion regarding the identity of the Messiah, God the Father ensured that Jesus' identity and purpose were made known thousands of years before He was born. He had to fulfill these numerous "impossible" prophecies so that all of us would understand that He is truly a sign from God and that He is God's solution to the inherent problems of mankind. Let me share with you a few of the numerous prophecies that have been literally fulfilled to authenticate Jesus' identity as the Messiah:

- *Virgin-born* prophecy in Isaiah 7:14 fulfilled in Luke 1:26-35
- *Birth in Bethlehem* prophecy in Micah 5:2 fulfilled in Matthew 2:1
- *Named Emmanuel* prophecy in Isaiah 7:14 fulfilled in Matthew 1:23
- *Ministry in Galilee* prophecy in Isaiah 9:1-2 fulfilled in Matthew 4:12-16
- *Triumphant entry* prophecy in Zechariah 9:9 fulfilled in Matthew 21:1-11
- *Betrayal by close friend* prophecy in Psalm 41:9 fulfilled in Matthew 26:20-25
- *Falsely accused* prophecy in Psalm 35:11 fulfilled in Matthew 26:59-68

- *Silent before His accuser* prophecy in Isaiah 53:7 fulfilled in Matthew 27:12-14
- *Pierced hands and feet* prophecy in Psalm 22:16 fulfilled in John 20:25
- *Crucified with robbers* prophecy in Isaiah 53:12 fulfilled in Matthew 27:38
- *Cast lots for His clothes* prophecy in Psalm 22:18 fulfilled in John 19:23-24
- *His bones not broken* prophecy in Psalm 34:20 fulfilled in John 19:34-36
- *Was thirsty on the cross* prophecy in Psalm 22:15 fulfilled in John 19:28
- *Burial* prophecy in Isaiah 53:9 fulfilled in Matthew 27:57-60

It is very interesting that specific details about Jesus' crucifixion in Isaiah 25:13-53:12 & Psalm 22 were documented hundreds of years before death on the cross as a form of execution was ever practiced. I submit to you that Jesus is not an ancient religious figure like Mohammed and Buddha; He is the Son of God.

::CHAPTER TWENTY-TWO

CHURCH
AND
STATE

Just as the identity of Jesus was misconstrued by many, so is the purpose of His Church misconstrued. People view the Church in many different ways depending on their profession, dispensation, needs, family values, mindset, or educational background. Some say the Church is just another institution like the Arts, Culture, and Literature. Others say it is the place to go when you need moral or spiritual adjustment. There is no doubt the Church is many things to many people.

The general lack of knowledge concerning the true identity and purpose of the Church has caused many people to have wrong perceptions about Salvation. At His departure, Jesus endued His disciples with the **Power** to continue His redemption feat to take back Civilization-the social, economic, and political kingdoms that were stolen from Adam and Eve by Satan.

In contemporary terms, Jesus' followers are to rule and reign as ambassadors of Christ in governments, businesses, and civic communities, to bring about God's righteous order in all spheres of life on earth. Therefore, true Christians are called to be **anointed** *judges, rulers, kings, presidents, government leaders, emperors, counselors, lawyers, business executives, directors, managers, workers, and individuals with wealth of influence, limitlessly industrious [with jurisdiction in sports, health/fitness, media, food and beverage, apparel, sales, maintenance/repairs, entertainment, science and technology, transportation, insurance, im-*

provements, real estate, construction, home making, bank-ing, finance, investments, etc] This is a true interpretation of the Great Commission (Matthew 28:18-20).

:: THE GREAT COMMISSION

The Great Commission is God's command for every true Christian to publish, distribute, announce, make public, broadcast, print, circulate, write, perform, establish, re-veal, administer, govern, visually display [through arts, crafts, dance, etc] and plainly demonstrate [by miracles, signs, and wonders] the reality of the Kingdom of God, with a view to changing lives, transforming the world, and bringing much glory to God (Matthew 28:18- 20 Mark 3:14-15 Mark 16:16-20 and Luke 24: 47-49).

It will take another book for me to fully explain how great a Commission this is, but based on the preceding explanation, you probably have noticed that the concept of separating Church and State is yet another demonic strategy to keep our social, economic, and political life secularized. The whole plot started with the institutional-ization of the Church. By the Scriptures, we understand that Jesus was not confined to a religious synagogue or limited to private spirituality:

Acts 10:38 *How God **anointed Jesus of Nazareth with the Holy Ghost and with power:** who went about doing good [effective and productive world-changing* *public services backed by the Holy Spirit], and healing all that were oppressed of the devil [casting out devils by the Power of God]; for God was with him.*

Jesus engaged in worthwhile public service and commands us to do same. In contemporary language, we can say that Jesus expressed His Faith in the Marketplace where He fed the hungry, healed the sick, counseled the depressed, released the oppressed, clothed the naked, provided for the poor, fought for justice for the weak, restored broken families, and taught biblical principles economics, government, and civic affairs. By the Great Commission, Jesus commanded His followers to reach-out to the nooks and crannies of the social, economic, and political arenas and restore people, places, and all things back to the Kingdom of God.

However, after His departure, the Church's public expression of the Faith was severely challenged. Thus, the Church settled for private spirituality and failed to fulfill the Great Commission.

:: INSTITUTIONALIZATION OF CHURCH

Whereas the Church is a people called out to continue with the *godly public service* that Jesus started, institutionalization has done a great disservice to this very purpose. We (the Church), somehow, allowed the world to define our identity and purpose. We got boxed-in and the tangible expression of our faith was greatly hindered. This prevented us from tapping into the great and awesome power of Jesus Christ that would have brought about great signs and wonders and miracles to change lives and transform the world. Thus, for centuries, the primary expression of our Faith has been nothing but religious rituals and duties confined to the sphere of private life; thus the expression *Private Spirituality.*

Instead of being a Public Power House, positively engaging the social, economic, and political life, the Church became a Private Powerless Institution, failing to bring worthwhile change and transformation to the world.

And so while most people view the State as a legitimate public institution, they suppose the Church is a private religious institution whose members have no business expressing faith in the social, economic, and political arenas. With such a mindset, it is very easy to view Church and State as two diametrically opposed institutions competing for power and space. Such negative perception has continued to fuel the growing tension between Church and State.

:: SEPARATING CHURCH AND STATE

America's first President, George Washington, said **it is impossible to govern America without the Bible.** I assure you that it is impossible for anyone to govern anything without the Bible.

Things visible are shadows or types of invisible eternal things. Life on earth was meant to mimic life in heaven; and human governments were meant to be visible expressions of God's Government in Heaven. But because of the sin of the first Adam, the States and everything else fell into the hands of Satan. But the Church was born to save civilization from generational destruction:

> **Proverbs 28:2** *For the transgression of a land many are the princes thereof: but by a man of understanding and knowledge the **state** thereof shall be prolonged.*

Jesus is the man of understanding and knowledge sent to restore the State. As God the Father sent Jesus the Son, so has Jesus the Son sent His followers to restore God's righteous order in the State and everything else pertaining to civilization. But for the lack of understanding, there really would have been no talk about separating Church and State in the first place. So to advocate separation of Church and State is a great disservice to God.

:: CAN THE WORLD TRUST JESUS' FOLLOWERS?

There is no doubt many denominations, sects, and many a so-called Christians have betrayed trust with the social, economic, and political communities. For that reason it may be somewhat difficult for people in the world to freely trust Jesus' followers or representatives to run the affairs of the State- governments, institutions, economies, etc. I also recognize the fact that many individuals and denominations, including the Catholic, have done things that are inexcusable. Many have used religion to manipulate the world and have done abominable things. I assure you that the Lord does not excuse religious atrocities; every deed will be accounted for before Him.

However, we cannot use the atrocities of men as an excuse to reject the Gospel of Salvation. Salvation transcends twisted denominational doctrines and fallacies that have misled many and destroyed much. The Bible says, "Let God be true, but every man a liar" (Romans 3:4). From Christianity to Islam, many are the atrocities of religious people; and many are their victims. But we must not allow past errors to negate our future destiny.

I also was a victim of religion. As a young man, I did not find any rest for my soul. Many Muslim clerics and church pastors lied to me, confused me, and cheated me. But Jesus did not allow them to destroy my destiny. Like Jacob, I experienced deep hurts in the hand of *the Labans* of this world, but the Lord was my refuge:

> **Genesis 31:7** *And your father hath deceived me, and changed my wages ten times; but God suffered him not to hurt (destroy) me.*

God is perfect; He cannot mistake you for someone else. He knows you personally, by name. Ask Him to come into your life, and He will meet you at your very point of need. He did it for me; He can do it for you too.

While I agree that there is a need to protect the integrity of the State from the negative influence of religion, I must warn that we refrain from mischaracterizing the Lordship of Jesus over Church and State. Jesus is the Centerpiece of God's plan for Civilization, State and Civic affairs inclusive. He is the Noah's Ark for this Age. Therefore, Church and State separatists should get some understanding of the Kingdom of God and refrain from castigating the work of God. For this work is not of men, but of God; and you cannot overthrow it; lest you are found guilty of fighting against God's will even for your own life (Act 5:38-39).

:: CHURCH AND STATE ADVOCATES

The motivation of many citizens who advocate separation of Church and State is not necessarily to protect the State from religious manipulation, but to protect their own selfish interests. Many simply want to compromise God's standard and secularize the State because they think that will excuse them from moral and spiritual responsibilities. Obviously such people lack knowledge. By and large, I have come to understand that many advocates of Church and State separation have two peculiarities:

- They do not understand Jesus' authority in heaven and in the earth; and so they'd rather keep the Church at bay, to avoid any possible conflict that might cost them their "liberty" and indulgences.

- They feel overly challenged by God's moral and spiritual standard. Concerned that their best efforts may never measure up, they do everything to keep the Church at bay to prevent the Light of God from revealing their weaknesses or rattle their *comfort zones.*

Please understand that there is none good. Even as Christ's followers, we are validated only by Jesus' finished work. The goodness that flows out of us into our communities is the Grace that the Lord generously pours out on us. Our purpose is to be an extension of God's grace in the social, economic, and political arenas of the world.

::CHAPTER TWENTY-TWO

THE LAST DAYS

:: FALSE PROPHECIES

I believe we are now living in an unprecedented time in history in which the world is slowly but surely dividing along religious line. And as this dividing line is becoming more and more apparent, international disputes are becoming more and more escalated. Many Arab nations are openly gearing up for a major conflict with the West, even as the thrust towards a nuclear showdown between Iran and United States continues to gather momentum. However, the United States remains defiant. President Bush continues to reaffirm his *strike-first* policy against terrorists and enemy nations, asserting that the administration's preference is to confront threats and halt the spread of nuclear and other heinous weapons before they fully materialize.

But the Bush administration is not alone in its doctrine of the *use of force before attacks occur.* Russia has been very busy, actively warming-up into the hearts of many anti-American nations in the Arab world. Iran, in particular, has been seriously emboldened by its alliance with Russia, and it seems it is only a matter of time before the rhetoric takes another dimension:

February 2006:
Iran's President Mahmoud Ahmadinejad, mocking the United States, calling it a "hollow superpower", vows to end voluntary cooperation with The International Atomic En-

ergy Agency (IAEA) and to begin enrichment of Uranium in pursuit of Iran's nuclear program regardless of whose ego is bruised.

For you to really understand that there is no amount of pressure from the U.S. or the international community that can stop the Iranians from completing their nuclear power program, you have to understand the religious ideology behind their quest:

President Mahmoud is said to be a pragmatic and smart person who believes deeply in the Shiite prophecy that the 12th Imam (the Mahdi) is the messiah who would return to save the "believers (Muslims)" and kill "the infidels (Christians and Jews/Zionists)".

The claim of this false prophecy is that we are in the last days, and the Mahdi will first appear in Mecca, and then Medina, conquering all of Arabia, Syria, and Iraq. He will then destroy Israel and set up a Global Islamic Government with headquarters in Iraq (Babylon). This false end-time prophecy *has essentially spurred* the activities of Iran's **Revolutionary Guards** and incited the current Iranian regime in its bid for nuclear power. It is very interesting that President Mahmoud Ahmadinejad publicly stated that this Islamic revolution would climax in the next two years, possibly 2008, coinciding with Iran's expected full *Nuclearization.*

There is a tremendous religious pressure on President Mahmoud Ahmadinejad to make this false prophecy happen as he believes that he is the forerunner to the Mahdi, the false messiah.

False prophets and false prophecies will play very crucial roles in the apocalyptic events relating to the final judgment of mankind in these last days.

Two thousand years ago, the devil set out on a mission to execute Jesus and put to death God's Salvation plan for mankind. But God caught Satan in his craftiness, for little did he (Satan) know that crucifying the Lord was indeed the very prophecy that had to be fulfilled in order to glorify Jesus. Satan fell right into the trap; for had he known it, he would not have crucified the Lord of glory (1Corinthians 2:8). By crucifying Jesus, he was in fact "helping" God's plan and prophecy to come to pass; for the Sovereign Lord taketh the wise in their own craftiness (Job 5:13).

Now history is about to repeat itself. Specific scriptures are about to play-out in unbelievable ways to fulfill specific prophecies. God will again catch Satan in his craftiness as he (Satan) attempts to use Islam and its associated false prophets and false prophecies to bring about apocalyptic events.

:: APOCALYPTIC EVENTS

Interestingly, 700 years before there ever was an Islamic religion, Jesus warned us about the false prophets who would come to deceive the world:

> **Matthew 24:3-5** *And as he sat upon the mount of Olives, the disciples came unto him privately, saying, Tell us, when shall these things be?* **And what shall be the sign of thy coming, and of the end of the world?** *And Jesus answered and said unto them, Take heed that no man deceive you. For many [false Christ or false Messiahs] shall come in my name, saying, I am Christ; and shall deceive many.*

Part of the signs of Jesus' second coming and of the end of the world is that a false prophet and a false messiah will arise:

> **Matthew 24:23-28** *Then if any man shall say unto you, Lo, here is Christ, or there; believe it not. For there shall arise* **false Christs,** *and* **false prophets,** *and shall shew great signs and wonders; insomuch that, if* **it were** *possible, they shall* **deceive the very elect.** *Behold, I have told...*

Scriptures continue to unfold even as the likes of President Ahmadinejad, Osama bin Laden, and many others, bound and brainwashed by religious spirits, become instruments of terror, dragging the whole world into an unprecedented war prophesied by the Prophet Joel:

> **Joel 2:30-31** *I will perform miracles in the sky above, and signs on the earth below-* **blood, and fire, and thick smoke.** *The sun will become dark, and the moon into blood, before the great and the terrible day of the LORD comes..*

One cannot call it mundane any explosion that causes blood to flow, fire to burn, and thick smoke to fill the sky. More so, when you consider a smoke thick enough to block sunlight and plunge an entire hemisphere into darkness. Only a major nuclear bomb explosion can perform such a feat. I am told that the super powers together now have enough nuclear weapons that can destroy the world many times over, and cause:

- **Blood of thousands of people to flow.**
- **Thermonuclear Fire to destroy cities, rendering nations unlivable.**
- **Thick Layer of Smoke, toxic gases, acids, debris, and vapors to fill the air, plunging an entire hemisphere into darkness. Thick layer may become prismatic to the point of refracting a weak sunlight not into a Rainbow (sign of Peace), but into a Crimson blood red color (sign of death).**

:: THERMONUCLEAR FIRE IN PROPHECY

In writing about the last days, the Prophet Joel foresees some gruesome scenes in which Agriculture/Livestock ceases as farmlands are completely wiped out, and the cities laid desolate. The *flames* burn up all the pastures of the wilderness and all the trees of the field. The heat from the flames is so great that it dries up the rivers of waters and completely destroy the vegetation; and all animals both small and great languishing, for the rivers of waters are dried up and the fire hath devoured the pastures of the wilderness (Joel 1:17-20).

Listen, thermonuclear fire does not scorch, it devours. Only a thermonuclear fire can do what the Prophet Joel foresaw. Yet, as deadly as this wrath will be, it is only an introduction- a preamble- to God's wrath. Please understand that these apocalyptic signals are also a warning to all Christian ministers, priests, popes, bishops, fathers, pastors, evangelists, teachers, prophets, apostles, and anyone else who may have already lost their Salvation or face the danger of losing it for perverting God's word.

:: BLOOD, FIRE, AND THICK SMOKE

Act 2:16-20 *But this is that which was spoken by the prophet Joel; And it shall come to pass **in the last days**, saith God, **I will pour out of my Spirit upon all flesh: and your sons and your daughters shall prophesy,***

*and your young men shall see visions, and your old
men shall dream dreams: And on my servants and on
my handmaidens I will pour out in those days of my
Spirit; and they shall prophesy: And I will shew wonders in heaven above, and signs in the earth beneath;
blood, and fire, and thick smoke: The sun shall be
turned into darkness, and the moon into blood, before that great and notable day of the Lord come: And
it shall come to pass, that whosoever shall call on the
name of the Lord shall be saved.*

The exact appearance of the moon depends on how
much dust, gases, acids, and clouds are present in Earth's
atmosphere. As total eclipses tend to be very dark after major volcanic eruptions because volcanic eruption
dumps large amounts of volcanic ash into Earth's atmosphere, so will an explosion from a nuclear bomb dump
unbelievable amount of smoke, dusts, gases, ashes, and
other elements in the atmosphere, enough to shield the
Moon from the light of the Sun.

While the Moon remains shielded, indirect sunlight still
manages to reach and illuminate it, but not without first
passing through the prismatic layer of thick smoke with
its filtering and refracting effect. It refracts the light into
different colors- *the Spectrum*; and then filters out most
of the colors except the red, orange, and yellow; the combination of which gives the moon a blood-red color. The
more dust in the atmosphere, the more red the moon.

You may have noticed from the apocalyptic events enumerated in Acts 2:16-20 that before the **blood, and fire, and thick smoke,** there will be a supernatural outpouring from God's Spirit, precisely timed and perfectly orchestrated to prepare the nations for the inevitable. Let me briefly enumerate this outpouring:

• **General Outpouring:** God says He will pour out from His Spirit, gifts upon every willing person who puts his hope and trust in Jesus. With the Holy Spirit working in them and through them, these true Children of God become equipped with God's power, wisdom, and gifts to understand mysteries and have insights to prophetic times, seasons, and signals. Depending on their assignment and calling, they will either dream dreams, see visions, and/or prophesy to varied degrees/dimensions.

• **Specific Empowerment:** Now there will be also a specific outpouring in which God will handpick His servants and specifically anoint them to accomplish strategic tasks and carry specific messages to the ends of the earth. Thus the dreams, visions, prophetic insights, and abilities that I have demonstrated in this book were made possible only because the Father has specifically anointed me for this specific message. In the same manner, others shall be specifically commissioned to proclaim the end-times message at different levels and dimensions. These specific servants of God are called to fearlessly shine forth as the light of God in the dark alleys of the social, economic, and political arenas of the world. We are not to fear for our lives because we have already overcome the adversary by the blood of the Lamb.

We are called to be passionate and bold, doing everything we can to turn many hearts back to the Lord and save millions of people from God's wrath. We are the prophets to blow the trumpet and announce that the worst nuclear nightmare, inconceivable by man, is about to happen. A very difficult assignment indeed.

• **Salvation Galore:** Now as these prophetic messages go forth with signs and wonders following, the grace of God shall abound for many to repent and be saved. Revival shall break-forth, and billions of people shall be saved.

Again, the call to repentance is not only to the heathens. It is also to those of us who claim to know the Lord, but do not do His will. Remember, the word of the Lord to you and me is that whosoever shall call on the name of the Lord shall be saved.

Please understand that what I am sharing with you in this book is the wisdom of God in a mystery, *even* the hidden *wisdom*, which none of the judges, princes, philosophers, intellectuals, queens, kings, and scholars of this world knew. For the wisdom of this world is foolishness with God. God's wisdom, ordained before the world, is now unraveling unto our glory in this Century (1 Corinthians

2:7; 3:19). Blessed are you, therefore, who read and hear the words of this prophecy, and keep those things which are written therein: for the time is at hand (Revelation 1:3). Let there be no doubt in your mind that even the imminent plot to annihilate Israel and destroy America is indeed part of the signs that the end of the world is just around the corner.

::CHAPTER TWENTY-FOUR

IRAN'S QUEST FOR NUCLEAR POWER

As the war of words between America's George W. Bush and Iran's Mahmoud Ahmadinejad continue to intensify, the longstanding rift between Washington and Tehran continue to edge towards red alert. Dated as far back as the 1950's, America's history with Iran has been nothing but trouble. Consider this:

- 1950's: under President Eisenhower, a CIA-backed coup restored pro-America Shah to power in Iran in 1953.
- 1960's: with America's help, the Ayatollah Khomeini was exiled from Iran.
- 1970's: the Islamic revolution toppled the U.S-assisted Shah, and Khomeini was restored to power. Khomeini then humiliated the U.S. government by holding 52 Americans hostage for 444 days.
- 1980's: U.S. supported Iraq's Saddam Hussein in his war against Iran.
- 2000's: as the war in Iraq rages on, the White House is accusing Iran of sabotaging U.S. efforts to stabilize the Middle East. Tehran, on the hand, is accusing the U.S. of promoting policies to toppling the regime and undermining the sovereignty of Iran.

Needless to say that *the West* and *the Middle East* are heading towards a major confrontation, President Ahmadinejad has now sworn that his country's chosen path- *Nuclearization-* is irreversible, and big powers like America should not make useless efforts to stop them.

:: IS AMERICA SAFE?

Physically, the nation seems much more secure; but spiritually, I sense that the door is still wide open. Although people in *the West* believe they are safe as long as Iran is not allowed to enrich enough Uranium to build a nuclear bomb, I want to remind us all that though we walk in the flesh (physical), our conflict against terrorism is not just a physical conflict. We are in a serious spiritual conflict against the stronghold of Islam; against the principalities, against powers, against the rulers of the darkness of this world, against religious wickedness in *high places*. Therefore, the effectual weapons for this kind of warfare are not carnal (worldly), but mighty through God to the pulling down of religious strongholds. America must therefore put on the whole armor (protective covering) of God if the nation is to survive this imminent ordeal and minimize casualties; for the evil day is coming, and is now here (2 Corinthians 10; Ephesians 6). The bottom-line is, a *Sword* has been raised against the *West*. The enemy is guaranteed to have the bomb; and he will surely attempt to use it.

:: WHAT IS AT STAKE?

Millions of lives, oil refineries, power plants, water plants, roads & bridges, waste systems, power grids, sea ports, air ports, chemical facilities, gas terminals, levees, dams, other civilian and military infrastructures; the economy, the political system, the banking system, information system, families, children, etc.

:: MOTIVATION OF THE ARABS

Apart from the false prophecy, the Arabs are also very uncomfortable with the U.S. "occupation" in Iraq because they believe that sooner or later, Iraq will be the base for the U.S. to launch attacks on Iran or any other nation in the Middle East. And with the U.S. currently building the largest military base ever in Iraq, it does not look like the U.S. is about to leave Iraq any time soon.

The consensus among the many Arab Muslims is that America is the great Satan fighting an unjust war against their Arab brothers in the Middle East; and that Israel is the small Satan fighting unjustly against their brothers in Palestine and   everywhere else. And so there is really nothing that will appease them except to see both America and Israel wiped out from the face of the earth.

What makes the current tension between *the Arab Muslims* and *the West* even more troubling is the fact that Russia and China are strategically capitalizing on the current fracas to enhance their military and diplomatic influence in the Arab world. Russia, in particular, is busy not only amassing more and more sophisticated nuclear weapons for its own arsenal, it is also selling them in great numbers to the Arab nations in the Middle East.

Russia's friendship with the Arabs, particularly its close ties with Iran and Syria is a sure sign that the massive and inconceivable **Russia-Arab Coalition** has already begun.

Historically, we know that the goal of the entire Arab Muslim world is to possess Jerusalem, because they believe Jerusalem is part of their inheritance. But for them to really possess Jerusalem, they will have to completely disable Israel. To succeed at that, they will have to first bring America to its knees. To achieve this goal, they need a super destructive force such as can only be generated by nuclear weapons, the expertise of which Russia is very glad to supply.

:: RUSSIA-ARAB ALLIANCE

We need to look out for two major Coalitions: *Russia-Arab Coalition* and *China-Russia-Arab Coalition*.

Why fear a Russia-Arab Coalition?
While the Arabs need Russia's help to achieve their goal, Russia needs the Arabs for a more strategic reason: *Three decades ago, America's Ronald Reagan accused Russia of making the world unsafe with nuclear weapons. In the aftermath of the Cold War, the Old Soviet Union (USSR) crumbled; Russia diminished, and America emerged as the foremost world Super Power. However, the table has now turned. Putin is now accusing the U.S. of making the world unsafe. Now Russia wants to lead and dominate the world*

again; and a nuclear bomb in the hands of radical anti-West Arabs is sure to set that desire in motion.

Earlier, I cited what I suppose is a mysterious coalition of a President and two individuals- who may very well be President Ahmadnejad and the fiery Ali Khamenei. Why? President Ahmadinejad and the fiery Grand Ayatollah Ali Khamenei are two Arab Muslims who have unequivocally declared their intention to wipe out Israel. Now I find it very interesting that these two are in very close military and diplomatic alliance with Russia's President Putin.

Interestingly, Russia's newly elected President Dmitry Medvedev has sworn to tow the same line as his mentor Putin. The 42-year-old Medvedev was Russia's first Deputy Prime Minister. Now he replaces President Putin; and Putin will become Prime Minster. So tell me, is the stage set or not? Tell me, is this the coalition to fear or is this the beginning of the coalition of all coalitions?

:: FUTURE WAR AND BIBLICAL PROPHECY

2500 years ago, the Prophet Ezekiel prophesied the future war of the nations- the war of all wars- set to happen in this 21st-Century. According to the 38th & 39th chapters of the book of Ezekiel, the stage is now set and the dots are now connecting:

Ezekiel 38:14 *Therefore, son of man, prophesy and say unto Gog, Thus saith the Lord GOD; In that day when my people of Israel dwelleth safely, shalt thou not know it?*

Ezekiel 38:16 *And thou shalt come up against my people of Israel, as a cloud to cover the land; it shall be in the latter days, and I will bring thee against my land, that the heathen may know me, when I shall be sanctified in thee, O Gog, before their eyes.*

Ezekiel 38:18 *And it shall come to pass at the same time when Gog shall come against the land of Israel, saith the Lord GOD, **that** my fury shall come up in my face.*

Today, specific nations and leaders in this prophecy are now emerging and joining in an unprecedented alliance to wipe out Israel from the face of the earth just as the prophecy had foretold. According to the prophecy, a Russian dictator will get into an unprecedented alliance with Iran (Persia) and other Arab nations. This sets the stage for the formidable **Russia-Arab Coalition**, and our mystery President may very well be Putin. Putin has already set the ball rolling. He has equipped Iran's President Mahmoud Ahmadinejad with ICBMs and he is currently arming him with a nuclear facility. All Ahmadinejad has to do is tip his ICBMs with nuclear weapons, and the rest is history.

The Russia-China-Arab Coalition is expected to materialize soon. China is currently spending heavily on military hardware- acquiring submarines, satellite killer missiles, fighter planes, etc for its army of 2.3 million soldiers. It is obvious that China and Russia are not preparing for minor regional roles in Asia or Europe; they are aiming to play global roles in the anticipated full-scale Apocalyptic World War. Thus the stage is set for the nuclear bomb explosion and the devastations that the Lord has revealed to me via dreams and visions. But there is hope: Jesus Christ the Son of the Living God died that those who choose to take refuge in Him may not die but have life everlasting.

::CHAPTER TWENTY-FIVE

ARE YOU READY?

:: THE KATRINA BLUNDER

Sunday, August 28, 2005:
The hurricane Katrina, still 14 hours away, had begun to announce its arrival as the seawaters powerfully surged against the shores of the Gulf Coast. Meanwhile the Lake Pontchartrain was fast rising and eating away at the base of the levee, which was the concrete floodwall built to protect the City of New Orleans from flood. By the morning of Tuesday August 30, 2005, the levee had given way and water had begun to flood the City at an unimaginable rate. Katrina indeed devastated cities in Alabama, Florida, and Mississippi, plunging hundreds of thousands of families into unspeakable agonies. But the damage done to the city of New Orleans in Louisiana, and the chaos and despair it brought to hundreds of thousands of New Orleanians is beyond imagination.

But was Katrina a surprise? No. Katrina announced itself before arrival. There was an obvious failure in the preparation and response to the Katrina crises. Many days before it plunged New Orleans into agony, government officials (federal, state, local, and other delegated authorities) were well aware of the looming disaster.

Between Thursday August 25 and Friday August 26, long before Katrina hit the Gulf Coast (that Monday) government agents had enough time to evacuate the innocent poor and weak citizens of New Orleans, but did not.

:: SO WHAT WENT WRONG?

On Monday the 29th, the storm slammed into the Gulf Coast, and a national chaos ensued. The fiasco that the whole world watched on television on August 30 (following the breaches in the levees and the catastrophic flooding of 80% of the City of New Orleans) reflected a botched relief and rescue operations that consumed 3000 lives and billions of taxpayers dollars. From the federal level to State and local, there was an obvious lack of coordination among the agencies involved.

In addition, the animosity between **Louisiana's Governor Kathleen Blanco and New Orleans Mayor Ray Nagin** made things worse. Their infighting was so grave that the Governor and the Mayor could not sit down together to work out their differences in order to save lives and properties, and protect the dignity of their people. It is not surprising therefore that the hundreds of buses meant to evacuate the poor and needy had no drivers.

Former director of FEMA (Federal Emergency Management Agency), Michael Brown, admits before the US Congress that the FEMA's response and rescue operation was a little too late because FEMA had logistics failure. "Logistics Failure" is a clever phrase by which government officials explain away their wrongdoings without really taking responsibility.

In the case of Katrina, this failure was fueled more by power tussles among the government officials involved in the *preparation, prevention, and rescue operations.* Unfortunately, bureaucracy has no respect or sense of urgency where the lives and dignity of **innocent weak poor and needy** families are concerned. That was why Colonel Tim Tarchick of the 920th Rescue Wing, Air Force Command was forced to wait 24 hours for permission to take his three rescue helicopters into the disaster zone. Can you imagine that!

According to *Newsweek* **Magazine**, September 12, 2005, Tarchick was unable to cut through the red tape until 4:00 p.m. the following day. By then the surging waters, up to 12 feet deep, had swept through the city. With hundreds dead, and hundreds of thousands displaced; and homes and businesses destroyed, there is no telling what Colonel Tarchick and the likes of him would have done to alleviate the plights of the victims had they been authorized early enough.

:: KATRINA TODAY, BOMB TOMORROW

Katrina was clearly one of the worst disasters to hit America. While many people heeded the warning to evacuate the cities, left behind were mostly *the poor no-car, no-money, and no-credit card people* who could not afford the cost of evacuation.

Their eventual evacuation to the super-dome was un-planned and uncoordinated. One chaos followed the other: *no food, no water, no bathrooms, no organization, no air conditioning, no lights, no structure, and no security.* Feces and urine smeared the walls and floors. Medical relief arrived too late. Dead bodies were all over the place. There were reports of gunfire and looting. By the end of the first week of September, there were a million Katrina victims without homes, jobs, or schools. One thing that bothers many people still is that tens of thousands of body bags [*for carrying dead bodies*] found their way to the disaster zone four days before food and water did; I guess logistics favored their timely arrival.

:: A FAILED SYSTEM

For days, government officials fought like cats and mice *over chain of command- who should be in charge and who should not.* Thus the exhausted families and helpless starving children found themselves at the mercy of a failed system.

The consensus is that, from the White House to the New Orleans' State and Local Governments, the whole system failed New Orleanians, the American people, and the whole world.

Fingers pointed in all directions: President Bush's critics say that he was disengaged, vacationing, distracted, and insensitive to the plights of poor black people. The White House fires back, blaming everybody else. Nevertheless, Katrina did more than to expose the vulnerability of a great nation. It exposed a great but imperfect system at various divisions and levels of the U.S. government.

Katrina exposed the magnitude of poverty amid plenty in America. The ghastly images of thousands of people mostly poor and underprivileged African Americans, crying out for *food, water,* and *rescue* is a reflection of a racially divided and class segregated America. Indeed Katrina exposed the serious need for America to seek the face of God. Therefore, government institutions must understand that God is sovereign over all things, even State. Politicians, diplomats, bureaucrats, administrators, and others must be willing to make a paradigm shift where Church and State relationship is concerned; for God is Lord over all things.

:: IS THE CHURCH READY?

It took FEMA 4 days to get to the disaster zone. It took President Bush 5 days. How long did it take the Church?

Katrina also exposed the Church's unpreparedness to respond decisively to communal, regional, national, and international crises. The Lord wants me to tell His Church world-wide that we are to be the first responders, as this is key to the end-times harvest. Katrina in New Orleans is a microcosm of what may happen in the future. I assure you the Lord is holding back the hand of the enemy because the Church is not ready for a great and sudden influx of people; and is unprepared to meet the great need that will ensue. With *9/11*, the people came and left because the Church was not ready for them. With Katrina, they came and left because the Church was not prepared. Now I perceive there will be a surge, but the Church must be ready. For this is key to the revival many have been praying for. He who has ear let him ear what the Spirit is saying to the Church.

:: PERILOUS TIMES

The time in which we live now should not surprise anyone; for the Bible has rightly prophesied in 2 Timothy 3:1-4 that in the last days, perilous times [dangerous, unsafe, terrifying times] shall come.

For this reason the Lord told me to tell His Church to get ready with the word of God and material resources to meet emergency needs because there will be many disasters. Today, about 94% of most church's resources go into administration while less than 2% is goes to missions and outreach to the poor and needy. This old mindset and ungodly prioritization must rapidly shift in order for us to accommodate real emergencies and adequately prepare for the task ahead. I therefore urge all true ministers of the Gospel of Jesus to set up the following departments in their establishments:

• **First Responders Team** trained and equipped with the Word of God, food, clothes, medical supplies, and other resources to stand-guard as watchmen over the nations; to tackle emergency situations when they arise.

• **Prayer and Intercessory Team** equipped with the truth of God's word to take on principalities and powers in various dimensions and regions of America, Middle-East, and the rest of the world.

• **A Missions Team** to keep the church on track so that we are not sidetracked by religion, but focused on our purpose and mission to restore the social, economic, and political arenas of life. A mission not to be traded for anything else.

• **Educational and Informational Systems** such that can help inform (in real time) and empower congregations, associations, businesses, and the general public to reach-out in the love of Christ (without prejudice) to the Muslims, Hindus, etc.

Whether we call them natural disasters or man-made calamities, the last-days prophecies are about to be fulfilled. These things will surely happen, without fail. The question is, are you ready for whatever happens, here or hereafter? Jesus, the Son of the living God, has already given us the Victory. I encourage you to receive Him and be empowered by the Holy Spirit to transform your life and make the world a better place.

Thank you, God bless you.

APPENDIX

BIBLIOGRAPHY

• Faith-Based Initiative Official Document: Guidance to Faith-Based & Community Organizations on Partnering with the federal Government. /FBCI.GOV.

• Duty of Hope: Armies of Compassion- A Bush for President Position Paper.

• The Texas Record: Governor George W Bush's Faith-Based Task Force.

• Urban Institute Research Paper Publication #407397 By Elizabeth T. Boris.

• The New Nonprofit Almanac & Desk for Figure/Notes on ES1/ES2.

• Reference book (the essential facts and figures for managers, researchers, and volunteers) Published by Independent Sector and Urban Institute.

• The Georgia Center for Nonprofits: On information published by Independent Sector, and the IRS master files.

• Africa's poverty profile: Developing Nations' social crisis: careusa.org.

• The Guardian, July 26, 2002.

• The Guardian Online; "UNDP report ranks Nigeria 26th poorest country," July 26, 2002.

• The United Nations Development Program: Confer ence Report on "Poverty Reduction Strategies: What have we learned?" Bergen, Norway 15-17 March 2001.

- The United States Agency for International Development: Nigeria -"The Development Challenge;"/www.usaid.gov/country/afr/ng; (May 29, 2002).
- The World Bank Group: "Nigeria: Targeting communities for effective poverty alleviation." Findings: African Region, No 68, August 1996.
- Worldbank.org./data/wdi/2003.
- The United Nations AIDS Program (UNAIDS) 1999.
- The UNDP and Poverty Eradication -Sustainable Livelihood (SL); see www.onusidacations/Poverty.htm.
- Victor E. Dike, author of Democracy and Political Life in Nigeria [Zaria, Nigeria: Ahmadu University Press] 2001.
- Ndulo, Muna; "Democracy, Institution Building, and Poverty in Africa."
- Inclusion, Justice, and Poverty Reduction - Villa Borsig Workshop.
- Series (DSE), United Nations Development Programme (UNDP).
- Alleviating Poverty in Nigeria by Anthony Maduagwu (Toniman).
- Nation Master.Com on Nigeria: An estimated 250,000 died of AIDS in 1999.
- Seven (7) Biblical Principles for Success in the marketplace: Biblical Concept of Stewardship by Apostle (Dr.) Paul "Buddy" Crum.
- The Role of the Business Sector in the Development and Protection of Human Rights. Peter D. Sutherland, Chairman of British Petroleum.
- Africa's Population as being 1/10 of the world's: United

Nations Secretary General Koffi Anan at the commission on private sector and development.

- The Seattle Times article on Dr. Martin Luther King, Jr. and the Civil Rights Movement: I've Been to the Mountaintop; In support of the striking sanitation workers at Mason Temple in Memphis, Tenn., on April 3, 1968 - the day before he was assassinated.
- The Seattle Times article on Dr. Martin Luther King, Jr. and the Civil Rights Movement.
- American Presidency.org: life/work of President Lyndon Johnson.
- 1997 Economic Census: Summary Statistics for United States 1997 NAICS Basis (for arts, entertainment, recreation...)
- History of the Church: Dr. Bill Hamon's Eternal Church, page 120.
- Financial Times of London: Article on President Da Silva of Brazil.
- Wesbter's Collegiate Dictionary (10th Edition).
- Strong's Bible Dictionary/On-Line Greek Bible lexicon: for the meaning of Hebrew language-based words.
- Edmund P. Clowny- The Church- contours of Christian theology, page 93.
- Dictionary of Ecumenical Movement (World Council of Churches) Publications.
- James D. Cantelon- Simply God- everyday theology for everyday people (on Gnostics and Gnosticism).
- Henry Chadwick- The Early Church- The Penguin History of the Church, pages 33-67.
- Richard Osborne- Philosophy for beginners.

- A History of Christianity- Vol. 1, the early and Medieval Church; Ray C. Petry, Editor.
- New 20th Century Encyclopedia of Religious Knowledge Second Edition. J. D. Douglas- General Editor.
- The Word in Life Study Bible (NKJV) Published by Nelson.
- A more Excellent Way by Dr. Henry Wright.
- The Ten Offenses by Pat Robertson.
- Understanding the dreams you dream: Biblical keys for hearing God's voice in the night (New/Revised) by Ira Milligan.
- Martin Luther: The Movie.
- The final messenger: Christ the final word by As Sayyid Issa Al Haddi Al Mahdi.
- CNN on International Terrorism.
- msnbc.com on International Terrorism.
- Jerusalem Coutdown by John Hagee on unveiling Islam.
- The Economist Magazine (Feb. 16, 2007): Next Step Ian?
- U.S. News & World Report Magazine (Feb 19, 2007): on U.S.-Iraq News
- NewsMax (Feb 2007): Reports on China's military arsenal.
- Global Exploits' Voice of Freedom February Bulletin.
- Wilkipedia: Supreme Leader of Iran.
- The Guardian: Inter-continental Ballistic Missiles.

ABOUT THE AUTHOR

Majority of people in the world today believe that Faith in Jesus Christ is neither practical nor relevant to public life. But God has raised up Segun Masha as an Apostle and Prophet to demonstrate the practicality and relevance of the Kingdom of God in the social, economic, and political arenas.

A Business Consultant, and a Certified Financial Instructor, Segun is a 1985 Biochemistry graduate of the University of Ibadan (Nigeria). He also served many years in the Money & Capital Markets of the Investment Banking sector. A Marketplace Minister, he strategizes to restore righteousness, equity, and justice in the social, economic, and political sectors. He offers faith-based solutions to the world's Social, Economic, and Political crises. In 1995, He was visited by the Lord Jesus Christ who commissioned him to bring change and transformation to both the Church nation and the world nations. Masha is to help bring liberty to Nigeria, and liberate Africa from the bondage of religion, poverty, and corruption.

Masha understands that the body of Christ will never change or transform the world unless Faith translates into tangible products and services to impact lives and communities. Thus he is raising up the Jesus Generation politicians, biblical economists, and biblical diplomats that will bring change and transformation to the social, economic, and political arenas of the world.

Segun Masha formerly repented and accepted Jesus Christ as Lord and Savior at the age of 22; and afterwards baptized with *The Holy Ghost and Fire.*

Please send your comments and questions to:
terrorunprecedented@hotmail.com